Supper with Rosie

Supper with Rosie

Recipes from family, friends and
far-flung places

Rosie Lovell

Photography by Georgia Glynn Smith

Kyle Books

Dedication
To my grandmother, Bunty Richardson, a fiercely inspiring woman.

First published in Great Britain in 2012 by
Kyle Books
an imprint of Kyle Cathie Limited
23, Howland Street
London W1T 4AY
general.enquiries@kylebooks.com
www.kylebooks.com

 ISBN: 978 0 85783 053 1

A CIP catalogue record for this title is available from the British Library

10 9 8 7 6 5 4 3 2 1

Editor: Vicky Orchard
Design: Ed Grace
Photography: Georgia Glynn Smith
Food Styling: Joss Herd
Props Styling: Nadine Tubbs
Copy editor: Catherine Ward
Production: Gemma John and Nic Jones

Colour reproduction by ALTA London
Printed in China by C & C Offset Printing Co.

Contents

Recipes to Remember

I learnt to cook in Suffolk among lentils, chickens in the garden, and really good, but frugal, ingredients. Vegetables grown (sometimes woody), herbs tended, but never much money spent by my parents. We ate fantastically. My mum's style was pretty unusual then. Deeply absorbed by Elizabeth David's recipes, she has always cooked a mix of southern French and Middle Eastern foods, and even now I am constantly on the phone to her, checking ingredients, memories and just chatting about what we are both cooking each night. And her mother in turn was a bit of a revolutionary cook in her time. Their home was more olive oil than salad cream, and more moussaka than shepherd's pie. And this was in the 1960s! My grandmother, Bunty, was brought up in the Pyrenees and travelled around Spain a lot. The foundations for my mum's style of cooking had already been laid.

Hoping to carry on what my mother taught me, I've mixed this with a healthy dose of city living for the last ten years, and I try and cook dishes from pretty much all over the globe, helped along the way by my very hungry husband, Raf. But the basis of my cooking comes from my mother. I'm hoping I've inherited her magical ability to season, spice and carefully plan every plate of food that comes from her kitchen. I can't deny that I aim to emulate her ways. I'm working on the gardening, but still have a lot to learn. And then there's my dad too. He was brought up in Jersey on a small farm, where they drank milk from their own cows, grew vegetables and suffered the seasons. My family is made up of my mum, my dad and my brother, and all we seem to do is exchange meals and food ideas. My brother, who lives in Kentucky and is a born-again American, often sends me photos of what he's been eating which usually revolves around hunks of meat. He cooks in a very different way to me, but our common and inherited love is food and the way it makes us feel – excited!

When I want comfort, I make a soothing noodle soup based on my father's love of making stocks, but modernised by the Asian aromatics that I find around me. And when my husband and I want a party we cook a mountain of different Indian dishes. Evolved and new recipes, but very much the same sentiment as my parents' banquets.

In my deli, I spend a lot of time talking to my regulars. While rolling out pastry (my mum's shortcrust usually) behind the counter, I chat away and always find myself talking about what we are all cooking and where each dish hails from. It's often our mothers. One of my original customers Dani for instance, who is very American, loves her family recipe for slow-cooked black beans. I stole the beans idea to go with a comforting belly pork dish. The family tree of recipes is always growing. I love the way my dad makes a Turkish pilau, and it is my starting point, but I've been doing it differently lately and adding barberries, caramelised onion and lamb.

My cooking was initially born as a family thing. I've tweaked the things I was taught along the way, through travel and living in a melting-pot city. I don't use exactly the same bread or chutney recipes as my mother, but the fact that we both cook these foods means that tradition is maintained, like glue binding us together. Nothing beats a laden foreign food market to get me thinking about new ways of cooking. Rice pudding? Try it with black rice and coconut milk. I've been really affected by time spent in India, Southeast Asia, Australia, France and the mayhem of London, and love that these new and exotic foods have infiltrated my Suffolk background. Recipes grow and change according to our families, friends, mood and fancy, and, frankly, what's in the fridge. Recipes have always been an ever-growing family tree of food. That is what makes cooking so comforting, so essential and so exciting.

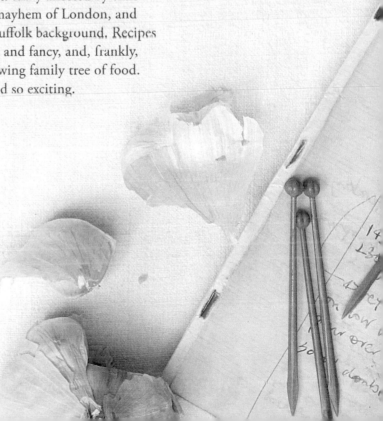

A Bowl of Comfort

When sick, most of us want our mum's food. Dishes that take us back to childhood and nurture, dishes that envelop us with the smells of home and the warmth of a hug. I always want soup. When it's good, it's wet and rehydrating, salty and full of flavour – something that will bring any poor soul back to life. There's a lot of mileage in a good soup, and if you make enough you can live on the cheap for a few days. It's not just for illness either, it's for comfort too. Soup is the only thing that really gets me warm when the evenings are cold and dark.

My dad was the keen soupmaker in our house. He was a cabinetmaker when we were younger and his workshop, which was piled with different coloured woods as well as lathes and chisels, was stalactite-freezing cold. A warming soup was exactly what he needed at lunchtime. For a soup to be really good, it needs a punchy, meat-based stock. My father was born when rationing was still in flow, so he hates waste and loves to utilise every last scrap of food. I learnt a lot from his pots of bubbling vegetables. Over the years I have adopted his stocks and broths and evolved them into other more multicultural dishes. These days I prefer a delicious chicken broth filled with Thai aromatics and rice noodles, or a proper tom yum soup made with the prawn shells to give that delicate coral-beaded base to the soup.

For the base of most European soups you will need onions, garlic, celery and carrots. Be sure that you always have some in the fridge.

Making a meaty stock is so easy. All you need to do is make a big pan with vegetables and aromatics and the meat or bones and put it on a low simmer for a couple of hours. I like to make stocks and jar them. Then your fridge will always hold the keys to a superior meal.

Soups are versatile. They can be clear and fresh, creamy and smooth, thick and chunky. The world of soups is never-ending, but do not confuse versatile with an undiscerning mish-mash.

French Onion Soup

This recipe is inspired by my best friend's mother, Felicity, a supreme home-maker. The first time I made this ancient French soup myself was really exciting; it is so simple (and cheap) and yet so delicious. The flavour all depends on you making a really good beef stock. I've added soy sauce to the stock, which is perhaps unusual, but it adds a nice salty injection to your broth.

Serves 4

For the beef stock

2kg beef bones (I use knuckle)
1 carrot, roughly chopped
1 onion, halved
2 celery sticks, roughly chopped
1 bay leaf
a handful of fresh thyme sprigs
1 teaspoon black peppercorns
4 juniper berries

For the soup

125g butter
800g onions, finely sliced
1 heaped tablespoon plain flour
½ teaspoon Worcestershire sauce
2 teaspoons soy sauce
1 teaspoon Marmite or yeast extract
30ml cooking brandy
freshly ground black pepper
Maldon sea salt

For the croûtons

8 slices of baguette, 2cm thick
2 tablespoons olive oil
2 teaspoons grainy Dijon mustard
150g Emmental cheese
50g Parmesan

For the stock, preheat the oven to 200°C/gas mark 6. Place the beef bones on a roasting tray in the oven for 1 hour or until they are browned, but not burnt. Transfer them to a large saucepan with a matching lid. Add the roughly chopped vegetables along with the herbs and spices. Cover with water and bring to the boil on a high heat. Place a lid on the pan, turn down the heat and simmer gently for 1–2 hours, depending on how much time you have. When it is ready, leave to cool slightly before draining through a sieve.

Melt the butter in a large pan over a moderate heat. When it has melted entirely, add the onions. Fully coat them in the melted butter and let them sizzle away for 15 minutes. They will first become translucent then sticky and brown. This is where you get the deep, delicious sweet flavours. Continue to brown, but not burn, turning often. Sprinkle in some plain flour and coat the onions. Pour in 1.5 litres beef stock and bring to a simmer. Add the Worcestershire sauce, soy sauce and Marmite or yeast extract and simmer gently for 30 minutes. Add the brandy and season to taste. Remove from the heat.

To make the croûtons, preheat the grill to high and heat a non-stick frying pan on a high heat. Brush the slices of bread with olive oil and place them in the pan – don't take your eye off the pan. (I've burnt them before by being cocky!) When they are really crisp and golden on both sides, remove them from the pan and brush the tops with a little mustard. Float the croûtons, mustard-side up, on the surface of the soup and grate over the cheeses. Place the saucepan under the grill for long enough to melt the cheese so that it is bubbling at the edges. Ladle into bowls, making sure each has at least one croûton.

Pea Soup with Shredded Ham

The British version of this soup was traditionally made with dried peas. I developed a yearning for pea and ham soup last year, but as frozen peas are not only cheap but super fresh I've used them instead. So sweet and yet so salty, this recipe is a perfect harmony of well-trodden flavours. Like French onion soup, it is one of those all-in-one soups where you make the stock from the meat ingredient in the soup, although you could use a leftover ham joint if you have one knocking around. This recipe is a great meal in a bowl so you won't want anything more to eat afterwards.

Serves 5 as a main or 10 in mugs

1.5kg smoked pork knuckle
4 medium carrots
6 juniper berries
1 bay leaf
1 teaspoon dill seeds
1 teaspoon black peppercorns
a few sprigs of fresh thyme
30g unsalted butter
1 onion, finely chopped
2 celery sticks, finely diced
1kg frozen garden peas
freshly ground black pepper

Soak the pork in cold water for at least 4 hours (this will draw out some of the salt). Rinse thoroughly and place in a medium pan. Cover with water and add 3 of the carrots, snapped in half, the juniper berries, bay leaf, dill seeds, peppercorns and thyme. Bring to the boil and then turn the heat to low. Simmer for 2 hours with the lid on. Remove the ham to a clean plate and strain the stock through a sieve into a clean pan. Set aside. When the ham is cool enough to handle, tease out all of the meat and shred using 2 forks – this will take a bit of manual labour. Take care to discard any fat. Tear the meat into fine strands and set aside on a plate for later.

Now for the pea soup. Melt the butter in a large saucepan over a moderate heat. When it is hot, add the finely chopped onion, the remaining carrot (finely chopped) and the celery. Stir to coat and then leave the vegetables to sweat for 15 minutes until they are softened. Add the peas (still frozen is fine), place a lid on the pan and heat gently for 5 minutes. Pour in enough ham stock, replace the lid and bring to a gentle boil. When the peas are just cooked but still fresh, turn the heat off. Blend with a handheld blender until silky smooth. Season with lots of freshly ground black pepper and serve with a nest of the shredded meat on top.

Aromatic Chicken Noodle Soup

Chicken soup, common in almost every kitchen across the world, has a reputation for healing, and this Thai version is no different. The chillies make for a full mind-blowing bowl of comfort that will cure you of any illness or lethargy. I fall back on this soup if ever I am full of cold or need a helping hand to recover from a heavy weekend. It is a very self-sufficient and satisfying soup to make. You make a stock first by combining your aromatics with some fresh chicken legs (which later get shredded into the soup) and then the broth is flavoured with a second set of fresh aromatics after it has been strained. As a result, the soup has a twofold layer of flavours, a serious double whammy of in-your-face invigoration.

Serves 2

For the stock

650g free-range chicken legs

4 small Asian shallots, halved

4 garlic cloves, peeled and roughly chopped

4 small bird's eye chillies, halved

1 stick of lemongrass, roughly chopped

5cm piece of fresh root ginger, roughly sliced

8 fresh lime leaves

For the soup

1 stick of lemongrass (woody outer layer removed), finely sliced

5 small bird's eye chillies, finely sliced

10 small Asian shallots, finely sliced

5cm piece of fresh root ginger, peeled and finely diced

6 lime leaves, finely sliced

200g pad Thai rice noodles

juice of 1 plump lime

1 teaspoon fish sauce

2 teaspoons light soy sauce

a handful of fresh coriander, ripped

First make the stock. Skin the chicken legs and trim off any excess fat. Place in a medium saucepan and entirely cover with water. Add to this the shallots, garlic, chillies, lemongrass, ginger and lime leaves. Place on a high heat and bring to the boil. Turn the heat down low, fit with a lid and simmer for about 30 minutes until the chicken is cooked and tender. Remove the chicken legs to a plate and set aside to cool. Strain the stock through a nylon sieve into a jug and discard the aromatics. When the chicken is cool enough to handle, strip all the meat off the legs and discard the bones.

To make the soup, place the stock back in a large pan. Bring to the boil and then reduce to a simmer. Add the lemongrass, chillies, shallots, ginger and lime leaves. Add the noodles and cook according to the instructions on the packet. When the noodles are tender, add the chicken pieces and season with lime juice, fish sauce and soy sauce. Serve in big bowls with some roughly torn coriander scattered over the top.

 If you have bought excess lemongrass or lime leaves, don't worry. Both of these ingredients freeze really well so you'll be ready next time the aromatic urge takes you. Make sure your stock is punchy. If you feel it needs more oomph, crumble in a little extra dried stock.

Cream of Tomato Soup

Tomato soup is the perfect childhood supper. This recipe is sweet from the uncharacteristic red pepper and smooth from all the arm-numbing blitzing. It is not complicated in flavours, but then again that's not always what you need. When I'm feeling really, really sorry for myself I can't take too many different ingredients going on in a bowl, so this is perfect for those times. I've taken to making this soup the day before, when I know in advance I'll not be getting much sleep. It's the ultimate lethargy cure. If you want to deviate from the old classic tomato soup add Thai basil for an aniseedy slant.

Serves 5 as a main or 10 in mugs

For the chicken stock

1 leftover chicken carcass

1 carrot, roughly chopped

1 onion, halved

2 celery sticks, roughly chopped

1 bay leaf

a handful of fresh thyme sprigs

1 teaspoon black peppercorns

For the soup

2 tablespoons olive oil

1 big red pepper, deseeded and finely chopped

1 onion, finely chopped

3 garlic cloves, peeled and crushed

5 large ripe plum tomatoes, roughly chopped

freshly ground black pepper

Maldon sea salt

1 teaspoon caster sugar

100ml whole milk

a handful of Italian or Thai basil, finely sliced

freshly grated Parmesan, to serve

rosemary oil, to serve

Place the chicken carcass in a large saucepan with all the other stock ingredients and cover with water. Place a lid on the saucepan and bring to the boil on a high heat. When it has come to the boil, turn the heat down low and place a lid on top. Simmer for 1–2 hours, depending on how much time you have – an hour would suffice, but any more is fantastic. When you are happy with your stock, strain it through a sieve into a large measuring jug and discard the bones. (I bag up the bones with all the other stock leftovers to avoid bad bin smells.)

To make the soup, warm the olive oil in a large, clean saucepan over a moderate heat. Add the pepper and cook for 10 minutes until it starts to soften, stirring from time to time. Then, in succession, add the onion, garlic and tomatoes. Soften for a few minutes and then place a lid on the pan and simmer over a low heat for 20 minutes until everything is nice and tender and it looks like a pasta sauce. Add 200ml chicken stock, bring to the boil and simmer for a further 20 minutes. Season to taste with black pepper, salt and sugar. When you are happy with your soup, take it off the heat and leave to cool slightly before blitzing with a handheld blender. Gradually add the milk, which will give your soup a clean but creamy texture. Ladle into soup bowls, garnish with some fresh basil and serve with a few shavings of Parmesan on top and a drizzle of rosemary oil. Suddenly, there is nothing boring about tomato soup!

Lemon Soba Soup

When I visited Tokyo I was bowled over by the new and exciting flavours I encountered. The nature of Japanese soups is very different to their European relations' and so I was keen to experiment. Where we naturally sauté the vegetables and then add hot stock, in Japan it is all about the stock. I have used a homemade miso as the base stock here. It is really easy to conjure and will give your soup a bona fide Japanese flavour. This method is entirely new to me and makes a welcome alternative. The result is light, healthy and lemon fresh.

Serves 2

For the broth

1.5 litres light vegetable stock
1 heaped tablespoon soya bean paste
1 teaspoon fish sauce
1 tablespoon Japanese soy sauce
1 tablespoon mirin paste
1 green chilli, pierced with a skewer
1 teaspoon castor sugar
1 teaspoon chilli oil with shrimp (available from Chinese supermarkets)

For the soup

2 eggs
1 teaspoon Japanese soy sauce
2 teaspoons vegetable oil
5g dried seaweed
200g sprouting broccoli, roughly chopped
100g enoki mushrooms, roots removed
100g baby spinach
250g buckwheat/soba noodles

To serve

3 small spring onions, finely chopped
zest of 1 lemon

To make the broth, place the vegetable stock in a large pan on a low heat. Add the soya bean paste, fish sauce, soy sauce, mirin paste, whole chilli, sugar and chilli oil. Let this gradually infuse for 30 minutes and try not to let it boil.

Beat one of the eggs into a mug and mix with ½ teaspoon soy sauce. Heat one teaspoon of the oil in a non-stick frying pan over a moderate heat. When it is really hot, turn the heat to low and add the beaten egg. Work it around the pan like a pancake so that it resembles a really slim omelette. When the edges are beginning to curl, flip the omelette over and cook the other side for a matter of seconds. Transfer to a plate while you cook the remaining omelette in the same way. Set aside while you finish the soup.

Taste the broth to check that it is well seasoned. Bring a large pan of water to the boil ready for the noodles. Add the seaweed to the broth, along with the broccoli, mushrooms and lastly the spinach. Simmer for 3–5 minutes, or until all the ingredients are well combined, and then turn off the heat. Drop the soba noodles into a pan of boiling water. Simmer for about 5 minutes so that they are tender but still slightly firm (refer to the packet instructions because cooking times vary). Meanwhile, finely slice the egg pancakes. Drain the noodles and nestle a bundle in the bottom of 2 deep bowls. Spoon over the action-packed broth and garnish with the sliced egg pancakes, some spring onion and the lemon zest.

Kentish Fish Stoup

This recipe is inspired by trips to the seaside where the fish is lovely and fresh. On my last visit I conjured this fish stoup because I wanted to make a really thick, hunky soup that involved using up all the fish remains as well, a bit like a French bouillabaisse. Stoup is a silly play on stew and soup, but describes this perfectly. It will warm even the most sea-breeze-beaten soul and the orange peel and saffron work wonderfully together to make this a little bit Moorish.

Makes 2 sturdy bowls

200g sea bream fillet, cut into 2cm chunks
200g coley fillet, cut into 2cm chunks
10 king prawns, shell on
100g squid, with tentacles

For the stock
1 celery stick, roughly chopped
1 carrot, roughly chopped
1 onion, halved
1 bay leaf
2 garlic cloves, crushed but left whole
1 teaspoon whole black peppercorns

For the stoup
4 tablespoons olive oil
1 red pepper, deseeded and finely diced
2 medium potatoes, peeled and finely diced
3 garlic cloves, peeled and crushed
1 onion, finely chopped
1 carrot, finely diced
1 celery stick, finely diced
3 tomatoes, finely diced
a good pinch of saffron
2.5cm strip of orange peel
2.5cm strip of lemon peel
lots of freshly ground black pepper
a good pinch of sea salt
1 teaspoon caster sugar
a handful of curly parsley, finely chopped

Make sure your fish is clean and then skin each piece. To make the fish stock, place the skins in a saucepan. Remove the heads from the prawns, along with their shells. Place the heads and shells in the pan with the fish skins and cover with water. Add the celery, carrot, onion, bay leaf, garlic cloves and peppercorns. Place the pan over a moderate heat and gradually bring to the boil. Simmer gently for a minimum of 30 minutes (up to an hour if you have time).

Meanwhile, remove the veins from the prawns under a running tap and set aside. To prepare the squid, slice the tentacles from the heads and place with the reserved fish. Chop off their heads and discard. Slice down one side of the body and remove and discard their innards. Finally, feel for their spine. Holding the tail, gently tug to remove. It looks like a shard of clear plastic. Clean under a running tap, slice them in two and score before adding to your fish pile.

To make the stoup, heat the olive oil in a large saucepan over a moderate heat. When it is sizzling hot, add the red pepper and potatoes. Fry for 10 minutes until they start to soften but don't let them brown. Stir frequently. Turn the heat to low and add the garlic, onion, carrot and celery. Sweat the vegetables for 10 minutes or so, stirring frequently, until they start to soften. Add the diced tomatoes, saffron, orange peel and lemon peel. Add enough fish stock to barely cover the vegetables. Bring to the boil, and then simmer gently for 30 minutes until the potatoes are really soft. Season thoroughly with pepper, salt and sugar. Drop the fish, prawns and squid into the stoup and poach gently for 5 minutes until the fish just starts to turn opaque. Scatter over the parsley and serve immediately.

Packed Vegetable Soup with a Creamy Poached Egg and Parmesan

This soup is a hearty rustic affair. The key here is to get your vegetables finely diced, add some good stock and the rest will follow. When you plunge into the poached egg, the yolk mixes with the broth and adds a velvet creaminess. For an extra kick, serve with some Chilli Sherry (see page 153) to splash over the top of your egg. Whilst the main components are well-worn European basics – onions, carrots, celery – I am not sure where the soup hails from. It was a recipe I developed when I lived in a very damp 1930s' flat and was constantly stuck with flu and in need of bowl-shaped love.

Serves 4

3 tablespoons olive oil
1 large potato, finely diced
1 small onion, finely chopped
1 carrot, finely diced
2 celery sticks (including leaves), finely
   diced
1 medium fennel bulb, finely diced
1 courgette, finely diced
1 leek, finely chopped
3 garlic cloves, peeled and crushed
2 bay leaves
1 teaspoon lemon thyme leaves (or use
   regular thyme)
3 plum tomatoes, finely diced
1.2 litres vegetable stock
sea salt
freshly ground black pepper
2 tablespoons white wine vinegar
4 free-range eggs
50g Parmesan

Heat the oil in a large pan over a moderate heat. Add the potato and let it fry for 10 minutes until it starts to turn translucent at the edges. Add the onion, carrot, celery, fennel, courgette and leek. Give everything a good stir to coat the vegetables in the oil, and then leave to sweat gently for about 10 minutes. Stir in the garlic, bay leaves, thyme and tomatoes and leave to sweat for a further 2–3 minutes. Add the vegetable stock and seasoning and bring to the boil. Simmer gently for 20 minutes until the vegetables are just cooked. Remove from the heat and taste to check the soup is well seasoned.

To cook the eggs, fill a large frying pan with water and add the vinegar. Place over a moderate heat until bubbles start to emerge on the surface (but the water is not boiling). Turn the heat down really low. Crack the eggs one at a time into a ramekin and gently ease them, one at a time, into the hot water. Let the eggs poach for 2–3 minutes, taking care not to let the water boil (or the eggs will break). When the eggs are cooked they will be firm to the touch, not too jellyish but not hard either. Remove them with a slotted spoon to some kitchen paper to absorb any excess water.

Serve the eggs nestled on top of the soup with a grating of Parmesan and a pinch of pepper and salt.

 This soup is meant to be fresh, so don't boil the vegetables to annihilation. You can change the balance or inclusion of vegetables according to the seasons. Throw in a handful of pasta and you have minestrone!

Asian Corn Chowder

This is a recipe that I got into when I realised how cheap corn on the cob is – especially from summer to autumn when it is in season. It's super-easy to slice off the cob and you can't beat it when it's combined, as it is here, with Asian aromatics and fresh turmeric. Chowder is originally a Scottish dish, which involves corn and potatoes, but by adding a few aromatics – fresh turmeric, chillies and ginger – the chowder becomes a totally different dish.

Serves 2–3

2 tablespoons vegetable oil

500g new potatoes, cut into 2cm dice

1 medium onion, finely chopped

2 bird's eye chillies, finely chopped

5cm piece of fresh root ginger, peeled and sliced into matchsticks

5cm piece of fresh turmeric, peeled and grated

2 garlic cloves, peeled and crushed

1 x 400g can coconut milk

3 corn on the cobs

100g green beans, trimmed and halved

100–200ml vegetable stock (optional)

sea salt

To serve

170g canned crab meat

5cm piece of fresh root ginger, peeled and sliced into matchsticks

a handful of fresh coriander, ripped

plenty of freshly ground black pepper

Heat the oil in a large saucepan over a moderate heat. Add the diced potatoes and fry for a few minutes before adding the onion. Fry together for about 5 minutes until the onion starts to soften, and then add the chillies, ginger, turmeric and garlic. Give everything a quick stir (but don't let anything brown), and then pour in the coconut milk. Place a lid on the pan and leave to simmer for 20 minutes until the potatoes start to soften. Meanwhile, cut the corn off the cobs and keep to one side. Add the green beans and the corn to the soup and pour in a little stock if you feel it is too thick. I like my chowder hearty and hunky, but it is up to you. Simmer until the corn is sweet and tender – about 5 minutes – and then season to taste with salt. Ladle the soup into bowls and serve each one with a little mound of crabmeat, some fresh ginger and a sprinkling of fresh coriander. Top with a generous shower of freshly ground black pepper to finish.

 Fresh turmeric is easy to find in Asian supermarkets and has a sour taste that balances the golden sweetness of the corn. If you are finding it hard to identify, look for a root similar to ginger but slightly pink. It may stain your hands when you peel it, so be prepared – I wear rubber gloves when I'm feeling vain!

Vegetable Stock

Vegetable stock is a core ingredient in so many recipes that it is worth offering a recipe, although anyone short of time will naturally use a pre-made one. The key to a European stock is the use of a nice fresh bouquet garni, a bundle of Provencal herbs. I love a healthy dose of allspice berries too, which add a deep and slightly tropical scent, being from the West Indies. And I've also added my mum's essential stock ingredient, juniper berries, the main component in gin.

Makes about 2 litres

3 carrots, roughly chopped
½ bunch celery, roughly chopped
2 onions, roughly chopped
3 garlic cloves, peeled and smashed
1 teaspoon whole fennel seeds
6 allspice berries
6 juniper berries
1 teaspoon black peppercorns
1 teaspoon sea salt
1 fresh bouquet garni
a squeeze of lemon juice
500ml white wine
2.5 litres water

Simply place all the ingredients in a large pan and place on a moderate heat. Bring the pan to the boil and then reduce to a simmer for at least 1 hour, preferably 2 hours. Taste to make sure that it has the desired punch. Depending on your taste you can add more salt. Strain the stock through a sieve and store in the fridge once cooled. It will last for a couple of days.

Brunch and Light Lunch

I quite often find that I get up late on the weekends, do a few domestic jobs and end up starving by two o'clock. Then there's a mad rush to find something to eat in the kitchen. It often loosely revolves around a fry-up: fried tomatoes on toast with garden basil leaves; some mushrooms with garlic and cream and hanging basket lemon thyme; scrambled eggs with some herbs from the yard. I discovered my new favourite way of eating boiled eggs because we'd run out of regular peppercorns. And you can't have eggs without pepper. I rummaged around in the spice drawer and found some little pinky-red, bead-like peppercorns that we'd used for salt-and-pepper squid. I crushed them in a pestle and mortar, and there you go. Szechuan peppercorns are perfect with eggs, giving a hot aniseed aftertaste. And, of course, there is the omelette! Any sort of omelette. You can call it a tortilla, or a frittata or an omelette. It's all good with me.

At other times, weekend lunches might involve a few friends or visitors who stayed over by accident from the night before. These occasions should be simple and picnicy and can be played around with too. For me, they usually revolve around an array of dishes, quick and abundant. As a child, our kitchen lunches were usually a mixture of leftovers and fresh food: Dad would make a few potato cakes with last night's mash, I'd make a few salads, my brother Olly would strip a roast chicken and Mum would oversee the seasoning and mastermind the whole meal. And in the summer it was always outside under the plum tree, where we would bat off the bees and perch in the shade. It was frugal and satisfying and I loved the mismatched foods and the sense of sharing with everyone passing around plates. I suppose what Mum and Dad taught me was that every occasion can be special as long as everyone mucks in.

When you are throwing together a quick lunch, the dishes don't all have to hail from the same place: a bowl of warm Scotch Bonnet Eggs, some Bianco de Trieste Courgettes and a big salad of 'Famous Red' would make a wicked spread. Don't get restricted.

Our brunches usually involve eggs. I can't resist their perfect nature. Whether you are scrambling duck eggs or making a rich decadent egg mayonnaise, they are one of the most satisfying ingredients around.

Amaranth Granola with Papaya and Yogurt

My cousins were brought up in America and the youngest, Rachel, has turned into a food connoisseur, making her own sourdough, granola and even roasting her own coffee beans. Rachel has recently very kindly advised me on the art of granola, a massively popular North American breakfast. I have added amaranth, a grain that I saw time and again in Mexico. It gives a delicious bite and is a high-altitude grain that's really high in protein. It bursts in the mouth and adds a great nutty texture. Served here with papaya, you will feel like you are on holiday.

Makes 20–30 servings

350g rolled oats

100g porridge oats

120g pumpkin seeds

150g amaranth seeds

250g whole peanuts (skin on)

125g pecans, roughly broken

120g soft dark brown sugar

2 teaspoons ground cinnamon

1 teaspoon ground ginger

1 teaspoon Maldon sea salt

125g date syrup

4 tablespoons runny honey

2 tablespoons vegetable oil

Preheat the oven to 150°C/gas mark 2. Mix the dry ingredients in a very large saucepan. In a measuring jug, beat together the syrup, honey, oil and 2 tablespoons water. Beat well with a fork, and then pour over the dry ingredients. Using a good spatula, stir everything together really well as if you were making flapjacks. Turn out onto a large baking tray with raised sides and spread out as best you can. Place in the oven for 45 minutes, removing the tray every 10 minutes to thoroughly turn and mix. Be careful the granola doesn't burn.

When the granola is ready it will be a deep golden brown. Remove it from the oven and immediately tip half of it out onto a separate baking tray to cool. (If you don't divide it when it comes out of the oven it will clump together in one large uncrackable piece.) Cool for 12 hours, and then jar up for your kitchen shelves. I eat mine with yogurt and my favourite holiday fruit, papaya.

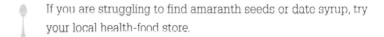 If you are struggling to find amaranth seeds or date syrup, try your local health-food store.

Poached Eggs and Asparagus with Hollandaise Sauce

My parents were never very pro-tradition, so for Christmas most years we devoured a big poached salmon with hollandaise sauce. As a result, I love this amazing fattening yellow sauce that is known for being difficult to cook. Hollandaise is my ultimate treat and if a bowl of it is placed in front of me, I may well eat it all. The richness is the very point. The well-worn combination of asparagus and hollandaise is hard to beat. Dip your asparagus in the hollandaise like you might dip chips in ketchup.

Serves 1 of me and 2 of you

For the quick hollandaise sauce
170g unsalted butter
1 tablespoon white wine vinegar
2 tablespoons lemon juice
1 bay leaf
8 green peppercorns
3 egg yolks

For the poached eggs and asparagus
1 bunch of new season asparagus
pinch of sea salt
2 free-range eggs
2 tablespoons white wine vinegar
freshly ground black pepper

Start with the hollandaise. Melt the butter in a small pan on a low heat. Meanwhile, place the vinegar, lemon juice, bay leaf and peppercorns in a separate pan and bring to the boil. Break the egg yolks into a medium mixing bowl. Strain the vinegar mixture a little at a time through a nylon sieve into the egg yolks, beating well with an electric hand mixer after each addition. Slowly pour in the melted butter, beating all the time until the sauce is thick and smooth. Set aside somewhere warm.

To prepare the asparagus, snap off the woody ends where they break naturally. Discard the woody bits and place the spears in a pan of cold water. Add a pinch of salt and bring to the boil. When the asparagus is boiling rapidly, remove it from the heat and drain immediately through a colander – this way, the asparagus will be al dente. If your asparagus is quite thick you might need to boil it for a little longer, but don't overcook it.

Fill a frying pan three-quarters full with water and add the vinegar. Place over a moderate heat. When the water is beginning to bubble gently, turn the heat down low. Crack one of the eggs into a ramekin and gently ease it into the water. Repeat with the other egg. Poach the eggs for about 3 minutes, keeping the heat low throughout. Remove the eggs when they are just firm. To test, scoop them out of the water with a slotted spoon and give them a good wobble. If they are still jellyish, pop them back in the water and leave them for slightly longer. Drain on kitchen paper.

Plate up the asparagus, place the eggs on top and pour over the quick hollandaise. Season with freshly ground black pepper.

Paddo Pots

Paddo pots were a revelation when I first discovered them. Deliriously weighed down by jet-lag, walking along a street in the Sydney-sunshine, I found a café called Tiger Mottle. They offered me a 'paddo pot' along with my creamy flat white coffee. It was an out of body experience, and made me sing inside. Now we make these often at Rosie's. They are really easy to assemble and don't take long in the oven. Ideal for a quick and feisty breakfast, make a batch of these and eat in your hands – a great play on the classic bacon and eggs fry-up and an all-in-one morsel too.

Makes 6

vegetable oil, for oiling
plain flour, for dusting
250g ready-rolled puff pastry
7 large free-range eggs
6 rashers of back bacon
freshly ground black pepper
sea salt
a handful of chives, finely chopped

Preheat the oven to 220°C/gas mark 7 and generously oil a 12-hole muffin tray, including the top surface as the pastry will touch this too. Dust your work surface with flour and open out the puff pastry. Slice into 6 equal 10cm squares with a long, sharp knife. Drop the squares of pastry into the muffin tray holes. Beat one of the eggs in a mug to make an eggwash and use to brush the edges of the pastry. Curl a rasher of bacon around the edge of each pastry case and then crack an egg inside. Looking from above, you should have an egg in the middle, framed with bacon and pastry. Season with pepper and salt and sprinkle over some chives. Place in the oven for an initial 10 minutes, and then turn down the heat to 180°C/gas mark 4 and bake for a further 10 minutes. Remove the paddo pots from the oven and leave to cool for a couple of minutes before releasing each of the pots with a palette knife. Serve warm on the hoof.

Soft Boiled Eggs on Toast with Szechuan Pepper

The first time I experienced this sort of pepper was on a visit to my favourite Szechuan restaurant in Hackney where their spicing is electrifying. Distinctly aniseedy, these brittle, dark red peppercorns are incredible. Eaten in large quantities they make me nonsensical – and yet, like an addict, I keep dragging more food off the mountainous table. Small quantities, as suggested here, will give your breakfast a whole new lease of life. This is a regular weekly breakfast for me, and it only seems to get better.

Serves 1

2 eggs
2 slices of hot, buttered toast
2 teaspoons whole Szechuan peppercorns
sea salt

Place a small saucepan of water on a high heat and bring to the boil. Lower the eggs into the water, being careful not to crack them on the base of the pan. Turn the heat down to moderate and simmer for 3½–4 minutes. Meanwhile, make your toast and butter generously. When the eggs are ready, plunge them into cold water to cool before peeling them under a running tap. Chop the warm eggs up onto your buttered toast. Finally, pinch the peppercorns between your fingertips to crush them (they should be quite chunky) and sprinkle over your eggs. Season with a pinch of sea salt.

I also add Szechuan peppercorns to omelettes, pâtés, pasta sauces and marinades.

Scrambled Duck Eggs with Basil Tomatoes

These scrambled eggs are made in the usual way, but instead of chicken eggs, I have used duck eggs. Bigger than the usual chicken egg, they are quite rich and have a slightly fishy tang (as they feed on fish). Scrambled, they cook beautifully and offer a fierce alternative to the standard fare. Cook them up with basil-rich tomatoes for a weekend brunch and you will feel like you are staying at a lush hotel.

Serves 2

For the tomatoes

2 tablespoons olive oil

300g cherry plum tomatoes

pinch of sugar

3 garlic cloves, peeled and finely chopped

a handful of basil, ripped up

For the eggs

20g butter

4 duck eggs

100ml whole milk

sea salt

freshly ground black pepper

To serve

4 slices of hot, buttered toast

Start with the tomatoes because they will take the longest to cook. Heat the olive oil in a frying pan on a high heat. When it is nearly smoking, turn the heat down to medium and throw in the tomatoes. Shake and toss the pan for a couple of minutes until the tomatoes spit and split and blister. Add the sugar, garlic and basil and leave on the heat for a further 2 minutes to allow the garlic and basil to infuse the tomatoes (don't let the garlic brown). Turn off the heat and set aside.

To scramble the duck eggs, heat the butter in a medium pan on a low heat. Meanwhile, beat the duck eggs with the milk in a bowl. Pour the eggs into the melted butter and, using a heatproof spatula (a kitchen essential), stir frequently until the egg thickens, taking care to gently scrape the bottom of the pan so the egg doesn't burn. As the egg thickens and draws together, take the pan off the heat and season with salt and pepper. Serve on hot, buttered toast.

Foraged Dandelion and Lardon Salad with Perfect Vinaigrette

This is one of the salads I knocked up when staying on a French Airstream campsite and it was such a hit I now let dandelions grow wild in my own back garden. They are delicious and delicate and a little bit peppery, at their best when you pick the young leaves (not the big woody ones). The dressing comes from my grandmother who was born in the Pyrenees and absorbed a lot of French cooking from her upbringing. She always cooked with olive oil and garlic, and this vinaigrette will definitely keep away the vampires.

Serves 2

1 tablespoon olive oil
100g prosciutto
2 garlic cloves, peeled
1 teaspoon sea salt
2 tablespoons extra virgin olive oil
½ tablespoon white wine vinegar
½ teaspoon caster sugar
100g young dandelion leaves, washed
150g 'Lollo Rosso' lettuce, washed

Heat the olive oil in a small frying pan over a high heat. Rip up the prosciutto into ribbons and drop them into the pan. Let these fry and crisp and become slightly golden, and then remove them from the pan to a plate.

To make my grandmother Bunty's perfect vinaigrette, take a small chopping board and finely chop the garlic with a sharp knife. Heap some sea salt over the garlic and, using the side of the knife, scrape the garlic and salt together until you have an oily paste. Scrape the paste off the board into a salad bowl. Mix in the extra virgin olive oil and vinegar and a little sugar. Add the leaves and crisp prosciutto and give everything a thorough toss, digging deep to make sure that all the leaves are coated.

My grandmother's trick for this dressing is to crush the garlic with salt to bring out the oils.

'Famous Red'

This salad is famous with my friends the Goddard brothers. It is fantastic for banquet-style summer barbecues. Joe Goddard made up the salad and his brother, Jazz, loves to eat it. It is big, soft, warm, sweet, and slightly meaty, a bit like its creator. You can make the salad with a classic French vinaigrette or with an Asian-style dressing including basil or parsley. I've opted for the Asian dressing here, using Thai basil for a deeper, sweeter flavour. Sweet and sharp and chunky, it is perfect served with some barbecued lamb or chicken.

Serves 4

1 green chilli

80ml rice vinegar

40g palm sugar or jaggery (available from good Asian supermarkets)

2 teaspoons fish sauce

2 tablespoons olive oil

3 red peppers, deseeded and roughly sliced into strips

200g lardons

250g cherry tomatoes

150g sunblush tomatoes

1 red onion

280g cooked beetroot

a handful of Thai basil or holy basil

To make the dressing, halve the chilli and place in a small saucepan with the vinegar, palm sugar and fish sauce. Set over a moderate heat until it has reduced by one-third. Leave to infuse, off the heat.

Meanwhile, heat the olive oil in a large, wide, non-stick frying pan. When it is piping hot, add the peppers and let them fry until they are slightly blistered, charred and quite soft. Turn down the heat and keep tossing the pan until they are tender and cooked – about 10–15 minutes. Tip into a wide salad bowl. Using the same pan, quickly fry the lardons until they are crisp and brown. Add to the salad bowl with the peppers.

Roughly chop the cherry tomatoes and sunblush tomatoes and throw them into the salad bowl. Slice the red onion into strips and chuck it in too. Chop the beetroot into rough chunks and add to the bowl with some roughly torn Thai basil. Pour over the warm dressing and get the meat off the barbecue to

You can make this without the lardons and fish sauce so that is suitable for both vegetarians and vegans.

Egg Mayonnaise with Chervil

I remember watching my mum when I was little, standing tall (on a chair) over her Kenwood mixer, blending this wondrous emulsion. Homemade mayonnaise is a little tart from the vinegar and unbelievably rich and addictive. My addition of chervil here adds a really delicate, fresh, liquorice flavour, which the eggs suit beautifully. It is one of my mum's favourite French herbs and is really easy to grow in a pot on the balcony. By using half mayonnaise and half yogurt here, you get a really nice light, tart dressing – a trick I learnt from my mother. Serve your egg mayonnaise with pickle-rich sidekicks – cornichons, anchovies and capers.

Serves 4

For the mayonnaise
4 egg yolks
1 teaspoon Maldon sea salt
coarsely ground black pepper
450ml vegetable oil
100ml extra virgin olive oil
4 teaspoons white wine vinegar
1 generous teaspoon Colman's mustard

For the eggs
4 eggs
2 tablespoons natural yogurt
a small handful of chervil, finely chopped

This mayonnaise recipe will make much more than you need to coat your eggs. You can store the remainder jarred in your fridge to slather on just about everything. However, if you wish you can halve the quantities.

Get everything ready for the mayonnaise. Place the egg yolks in a large mixing bowl and season with salt and pepper. Measure out the oils and place them together in a jug. Using a hand mixer, begin to slowly beat the yolks. Add just a tiny drip of the oil and continue beating. Continue adding the oil, one drip at a time, beating continuously until you have incorporated about one-third of it. The mixture should be really thick. I have added the oil too quickly in the past and it doesn't work; you have to be extremely measured. Once you have added one-third of the oil, add the vinegar to loosen the mixture. You can then pour in the rest of the oil more quickly, whisking all the time. Once all the oil has been incorporated, add the mustard and taste. The mayonnaise should be rich and creamy, but have a nice kick.

To cook the eggs, place them in a small saucepan and cover with water. Place the pan on a high heat and bring to the boil. Once the water comes to the boil, time 3 minutes on your egg timer. When the alarm goes off, turn off the heat immediately and fit a lid on the pan. Now set your timer for 8 minutes and leave the eggs to stand, off the heat. Drain the eggs under a cold running tap and keep them covered with cold water until you are ready to peel them – this way, the shell will come off easily and there will be no shredded edges in sight. Chop the eggs into quarters. To make the dressing, combine 2 tablespoons of your egg mayonnaise with the yogurt in a clean bowl. Season to taste. Fold the eggs carefully into the dressing, making sure you keep the yolks intact. Scatter some chervil over the top before serving.

Remoulade

Remoulade is a French staple, not unlike our coleslaw, being deliciously creamy and fresh at the same time. You can pick it up in the cold counter of any French supermarket. Homemade and served with a selection of salads and meats it makes a delicious lunch. Celeriac is the main ingredient here. It is a wonderful vegetable, celery-like, and in its raw form looks almost prehistoric and very muddy. I've added yogurt to cut the mayonnaise, which makes the remoulade much lighter and perhaps untraditional. It is my mum's trick for almost every egg-heavy dressing.

Serves 4

300g celeriac
juice of ½ lemon
1 heaped teaspoon mustard powder
1 teaspoon olive oil
1 tablespoon yogurt
1 tablespoon mayonnaise
1 heaped teaspoon grainy Dijon mustard
1 teaspoon caster sugar
freshly ground black pepper
½ teaspoon sea salt

Slice the rough skin and any knobbles off the celeriac. Grate coarsely – or, better still, julienne with a mandolin slicer for perfect shredding. Place in a bowl. Squeeze over the lemon juice and give the celeriac a good toss to stop it going brown. Set aside.

To make the dressing, measure out the mustard powder into a bowl, add the oil and mix to form a paste. Stir in the yogurt, mayonnaise, grainy mustard, sugar, pepper and salt. Taste in case it needs more seasoning, and then combine with the celeriac and serve.

If you want slightly more crunch, add in some finely sliced fennel and cut down on the celeriac.

Panzanella

A Florentine salad in origin, for me this recipe strongly evokes a great trip to Sydney, where I first made it. Ingredients in this heavenly city are abundant and vivid and thoroughly inspiring. Panzanella is all about assembling, which is easy, and mixing and matching. Best of all it uses stale bread, so it is super economical. The bread becomes moist from the wet, ripe tomatoes, making your spoils taste deliciously comforting, but also tart and summery. You can alternate the ingredients according to what is around. Sometimes I use feta, which is delicious and salty. You can also use mozzarella too.

Serves 5–6

450g yellow baby plum tomatoes, halved

450g red baby plum tomatoes, halved

1 medium red onion, finely sliced

40g fresh basil, ripped

280g stale ciabatta, ripped into chunks

100g capers in brine, drained

100g pitted black olives, halved

1 tablespoon red wine vinegar

3 tablespoons extra virgin olive oil

freshly ground black pepper

2 garlic cloves, peeled and crushed

½ teaspoon caster sugar

½ teaspoon sea salt

250g ricotta

Find a large mixing bowl and combine both the yellow and red tomatoes. Using your hands, gradually mix in the onion, basil, chunks of bread, capers and black olives. In a separate bowl, beat together the vinegar, oil, pepper, garlic, sugar and salt to make a dressing. Taste to check that it is well seasoned (but be aware it doesn't need to be too sharp because the tomatoes have their own acidity). Pour the dressing over the salad and combine thoroughly with your hands – by now the bread should be starting to soften from the dressing and the tomato juices. Tip the whole salad out onto a large serving dish and crumble over the ricotta. Leave for half an hour to allow the flavours to melge before serving.

 Don't make this salad too far in advance – the bread will become too rehydrated and you will end up with a pappy mess. My Australian-Italian friend, Adam dal Pozzo, recommends roasting the bread in an oven on a low heat first, so that it is nice and brittle.

Picnic Tandoori Chicken

In its truest form, tandoori chicken is marinated in yogurt and spices and roasted in a tandoor or clay oven. This recipe, a devolved version, is inspired by one of my mum's staple picnic dishes, whether we were in our garden or out for the day in the summer. She used drumsticks for their thrifty value, and caked in spicy yogurt, they are perfect caveman munching. I've added some more specific Indian aromatics here and good potent chillies that she may not have been able to get hold of when we were children.

Serves 4

900g chicken drumsticks (or a mix of
    drumsticks and thighs)
400g natural yogurt
4 large garlic cloves, peeled and crushed
5cm piece of fresh root ginger, peeled and
    grated
1 teaspoon hot Madras curry powder
3 teaspoons tandoori masala
1 teaspoon ground coriander
2 teaspoons ground turmeric
2 small green chillies, finely chopped
1 teaspoon freshly ground black pepper
2 teaspoons Maldon sea salt
a small handful of coriander, roughly
    ripped, to garnish

Skin the drumsticks by pulling the skin from the wide end over the bone. (If you are using thighs, skin these too.) Puncture each one a few times with a sharp knife and lay the pieces of chicken in a large baking tray. Mix up the marinade by beating together the yogurt with the garlic, ginger, spices, chillies and seasoning. Pour this over the chicken and give it a really good mix with your hands to coat the chicken all over. Leave to marinate in the fridge for a minimum of 3 hours, but preferably overnight.

Preheat the oven to 160°C/gas mark 3. Remove the chicken from the fridge and turn the pieces over to make sure they are caked really well in the yogurt. Place the baking tray in the oven for 1 hour 15 minutes, turning and basting once during this time. Remove from the oven and leave the chicken pieces to cool. Garnish with a little fresh coriander and serve warm or cold – both are delicious.

Scotch Bonnet Eggs

I got this tip off my friend Shola. Shola loves Scotch bonnet chillies and freely adds them to her meat shell. It works a treat. I avoided Scotch eggs for a good few years in fear of them being really hard work. They aren't I assure you. And the results are to die for. Make these for a picnic and you will be the favourite contributor.

Serves 4

4 large free-range eggs
290g sausagemeat
2 spring onions, finely chopped
½ Scotch bonnet, finely chopped
sea salt
freshly ground black pepper
½ teaspoon dried mixed herbs
150g freshly made breadcrumbs
1 large free-range egg, beaten
2 tablespoons plain flour
1 litre vegetable oil

Place the eggs in a pan of water and bring to the boil. Reduce the heat to moderate and simmer for 7 minutes exactly. I use a stopwatch to make sure I am on the dot. Immediately remove the pan from the heat and place the eggs under cold running water. Set these aside to cool in the cold water.

For the meat shell, thoroughly mix together the sausagemeat with the spring onions, Scotch bonnet, salt, pepper and dried herbs. Divide this into 4 equal parts. Stretch out some clingfilm on a chopping board and then place each patty on the clingfilm. Press down so that each makes a flat circle measuring about 10cm in diameter and layer another piece of clingfilm on top. Place these in the fridge while the eggs continue to cool.

After about half an hour, assemble the Scotch eggs by placing the breadcrumbs on one plate, the egg in a shallow bowl and the flour on another plate. Peel the eggs and roll them in the flour so that they are entirely coated. Press the sausagemeat around the eggs, using the clingfilm to help you fold it around them. Seal them completely, shaping in your palms. Now roll the eggs in the beaten egg and lastly the breadcrumbs. When you have followed this process with each of the eggs, heat the oil in a medium pan on a high heat. To check that the oil is ready, drop in a little of the remaining breadcrumbs. These should fizz energetically. Using a spoon, lower each of the eggs into the oil and let them fry. Move them gently around the pan so that they are cooked all over. They should become dark brown when ready – about 8–10 minutes. Remove using a slotted spoon to some kitchen paper to absorb any excess oil. These are best eaten warm out of the pan, so slice open as soon as you can handle them and munch in your hands.

Turbo Tzatziki

Tzatziki can be more than just yogurty cucumber. There are lots of additions you can make to this creamy dip to give depth of flavour. Some old friends, David and Sam, recently made a delicious raita but used courgette instead of cucumber, because that's what they had to hand. It got me thinking. It's all about maximum flavour here – going the extra mile. Add lots of garlic and roasted cumin and you turn an ordinary dish into a winner. I now make it all the time in the café.

Serves 6–8

2 small courgettes, grated
1 cucumber, peeled, deseeded and diced
6 radishes, trimmed and quartered
3 garlic cloves, peeled and crushed
3 spring onions, finely chopped
1 Mediterranean red chilli, finely chopped
30g fresh mint, finely chopped
30g fresh parsley, finely chopped
zest and juice of ½ lemon
7g whole cumin seeds
550g natural strained yogurt
2 tablespoons extra virgin olive oil
freshly ground black pepper
sea salt

Place the grated courgette and diced cucumber in a salad bowl. Add the quartered radishes, garlic, spring onions and chilli. Give it a good toss with your hands before adding the fresh mint and parsley. Grate in some lemon zest and then add some lemon juice to keep it fresh. Set aside.

Roast the cumin seeds in a dry frying pan over a low flame until their scent is emanating into the room. The seeds should be dancing in the pan. Remove the cumin from the pan to a plate immediately so that they don't burn. Leave to cool.

Mix two-thirds of the cumin seeds into the vegetables followed by the yogurt, olive oil and seasoning. Taste to make sure that it is punchy and add more seasoning if necessary. Spoon the tzatziki into a clean, shallow bowl and then scatter over the rest of the toasted cumin seeds. For extra beauty, drizzle over a little more olive oil. Serve with toasted pitta bread or finely sliced toasted ciabatta.

Chicken and Orange Tabbouleh

Tabbouleh is an Arabic salad, parsley-dominated, with bulgar wheat, tomatoes and herbs, which has been adopted in France and indeed all over the world. I love making this salad as it is such a hearty and filling summer feed. This version has bitter walnuts, fresh dill and moist leftover chicken. Whilst all the ingredients are classic Arabic components, they are not commonly used in the traditional tabbouleh recipe.

Serves 6

700g leftover roast chicken
300g medium bulgar wheat
500ml vegetable stock
120g walnuts
2 teaspoons cumin seeds
1 orange
2 tablespoons extra virgin olive oil
1 large mild chilli, finely chopped
2 garlic cloves, peeled and finely chopped
40g fresh dill, roughly chopped
2 teaspoons sea salt
1 leek (or red onion), finely sliced
80g fresh parsley, roughly chopped
juice of 1 lemon
2 tablespoons walnut oil

Strip the cooked chicken off the carcass. Measure the bulgar wheat into a large pan. Pour over enough stock to cover and place a lid on the pan. Put the pan on a very low heat for 5 minutes, and then remove from the heat and fluff up with a fork. Taste to check that it is cooked. If you think it is too gritty, replace the lid and leave to stand for a few minutes longer to allow it to cook in its own steam. Set aside.

Toast the walnuts and cumin seeds separately. This is best done in a dry frying pan on a low heat (watch them carefully because they will both burn easily). Tip onto a plate to cool.
Grate the zest off the orange into a pestle and mortar. Add to this the olive oil, chilli, garlic, dill and salt. Crush everything together to form a coarse paste, and then scoop the mixture into the bulgar wheat. Combine carefully with a fork. Remove the peel and pith from the orange with a sharp knife and cut the flesh into 1cm cubes. Add to the bulgar wheat with the leek (or red onion), the toasted walnuts and cumin seeds, the leftover chicken and the parsley. Squeeze over the lemon juice, add the walnut oil and mix carefully with your hands to combine. Season with a little more salt if necessary.

Spiced Cauliflower Salad

This salad is a bit of a coup. It was a combination of flavours that had been playing on my mind for a few weeks and I urgently needed to try it. Plus cauliflowers were all over the market taunting me! My friends Louise and Steph and I had planned a sunny Saturday lunch and this struck me as an ideal opportunity to try it out. We sat on Louise's roof terrace, bathed in sunshine, drinking crisp white wine and celebrated. It is the perfect full-bodied addition to a lunchtime spread.

Serves 4

600g fresh, firm cauliflower, divided into
    florets
4 tablespoons vegetable oil
1 medium white salad onion, finely sliced
1 Turkish green chilli, finely sliced
1 dried green chilli, snapped in half
3 teaspoons mustard seeds
2 teaspoons ground cumin
2 teaspoons ground turmeric
1 teaspoon ground cinnamon
1½ teaspoons ground coriander
sea salt
freshly ground black pepper
juice of 1–1½ lemons

Blanch the cauliflower by bringing it to the boil and simmering for just a few minutes. It should be still firm as it will be fried later down the line. Leave this in the water whilst you get on with the spicing.

Heat the oil in a large wide frying pan or wok on a high heat. Add the onion and chillies and fry until they just begin to brown and then turn the heat to low. Add the spices and coat the onion for a few minutes. Drain the cauliflower florets and then add to the frying pan for a few minutes, again coating with the spices thoroughly. Continue to heat and mix for a few minutes. Season the pan with lots of salt and pepper and squeeze over the lemon juice. Tip the salad out into a nice salad bowl or serving dish and let it cool for 10 minutes or so. Serve warm with some yogurt and flatbread.

Sticky Ribs with Chive Flower Potato Salad

These ribs are a mixture of many cuisines: a bit American (ketchup); a bit Asian (star anise); and a lot tasty (the date syrup is my latest addition). The essence of a good barbecued rib, which is prevalent in many cultures, is a hefty slathering of marinade and maximum surface area. They should be punchy, so pack your sauce full of flavours. You can mix and match the balance of ingredients too. The chive flowers give the salad its allium kick and this potato salad calls for a vinaigrette dressing, which is lighter than the usual mayo, to balance the strong flavours of the ribs.

Serves 4

For the ribs

1kg pork ribs
juice of 1 lime
3 tablespoons vegetable oil
2 tablespoons mushroom ketchup or
    brown sauce
4 tablespoons tomato ketchup
2 tablespoons soy sauce
2 tablespoons date syrup
2 teaspoons chilli flakes
6 whole star anise
2 teaspoons cumin seeds
1½ teaspoons allspice berries
7.5cm piece of fresh root ginger, peeled
    and grated
6 bird's eye chillies, finely chopped
5 garlic cloves, peeled and crushed
1 tablespoon caster sugar

For the salad

600g new potatoes, such as Jersey Royals,
    scrubbed and sliced in half
3 tablespoons olive oil
1 tablespoon tarragon vinegar
1 teaspoon smooth Dijon mustard
freshly ground black pepper
sea salt
a few sprigs of fresh mint, chopped
20 chive flowers

Divide the ribs between the bones using a sharp knife. Place them in a medium saucepan and cover with water. Bring to the boil and simmer on a lowish heat for 10 minutes. Drain well and tip into a large roasting tray.

To make the marinade, take a large measuring jug. Squeeze in the lime juice and add the vegetable oil. Beat in the 2 ketchups, soy sauce and the date syrup. Take a pestle and mortar, measure in the chilli flakes, star anise, cumin and allspice and grind to a fine powder. Pour this into the marinade and add the ginger, fresh chillies and garlic. Lastly mix in the sugar. Pour the marinade over the ribs and mix everything thoroughly with your hands. Set aside to marinate for 1 hour. Preheat the oven to 200°C/gas mark 6 or light your barbecue.

Bake your tray of ribs on the top shelf of the oven for an initial 30 minutes, and then remove and baste thoroughly. Turn down the heat to 150°C/gas mark 3, return the ribs to the oven and cook for a further 30 minutes. Alternatively, you can barbecue the ribs until they are crisp and dark.

To make the potato salad, place the potatoes in a medium pan and cover with water. Add a pinch of salt and bring to the boil. Simmer for about 30 minutes until the potatoes slip easily off a sharp knife. Drain the potatoes and let them cool for 20 minutes before adding the dressing. To make the dressing, place the oil, vinegar, mustard, pepper and salt in a jar. Place the lid on top and give everything a good shake. Turn your potatoes out into a nice salad bowl and pour over the dressing. Scatter with the mint and chive flowers.

Bianco di Trieste Courgettes with Sumac and Feta

I love these pale, tender courgettes. They are easy to find in Turkish neighbourhoods, and work really well baked. This is my perfect summer dish; add the sheep's feta once the courgettes are removed from the oven and watch the snow-like cheese melt and soften. It is very simple to make and can be ready in just under an hour, making it a great rustle-up lunch to serve with some bread, cold meat and chutneys.

Serves 4

3 medium 'bianco di Trieste' courgettes
2 tablespoons olive oil
1 heaped teaspoon sumac (available from Turkish and Greek stores)
1 teaspoon sea salt
freshly ground black pepper
2 tablespoons pine nuts
100g sheep's feta

Preheat the oven to 180°C/gas mark 4. Slice the courgettes in half lengthways, leaving the stalks on, and lay in a baking dish, flesh-side up. Pour over the olive oil, sprinkle with the sumac (which does the same job as lemon) and some salt and pepper. Bake in the oven for 45 minutes until the courgettes are browned and jammy. Meanwhile, warm a frying pan over a moderate heat. Add the pine nuts and toast in the dry pan, tossing frequently, until pale golden brown. Tip onto a plate to cool.

Remove the courgettes from the oven and crumble over the feta. Scatter the pine nuts over the top and leave to stand for 5–10 minutes to allow the courgettes to cool slightly and the cheese to soften. Taste for seasoning, adding more sumac if necessary to make it slightly sharper.

Weeknights In

When I cook during the week it tends to be a flying trip to the shops for fresh herbs and some extras and a quickly rustled nourishing feast. It often involves using up a little of what's left in the fridge, and falling back on familiar favourites. Frugality is a familial trait. These meals are not fussy or costly of time or money. My mum cooks with such ease I think my laid-back attitude is directly her fault!

I love the fact that midweek entertaining is an open-ended thing. It's a time when everyone is welcome. I recently cooked supper for my school friend Chloe and before we knew it another of our friends, Tash, had invited herself along too. Luckily I'd made a venison stew so it was easy to stretch. At home when I was a child everyone was always welcome. A few extra mouths to feed just meant a few extra hands for washing up. My mum can knock up a meal out of nothing and this is the essence of a simple midweek supper.

When we were little we had a lot of pasta dishes, baked potatoes and packed salads. One of the key lessons my mum passed onto me is how to make something out of nothing – a few tins of chickpeas and supper is all yours. Her favourite was pasta bake. Though less fashionable now, it was a great way of filling everyone up on a shoestring. Packed salads were always my favourite, though. A salad can be so much more than leaves. By toasting some sunflower seeds and making a tip-top dressing, salad becomes a meal in itself.

Simplicity is not a crime. Nor does it imply that you can't cook. Sometimes the simple things, so long as they are well devised and sensitively constructed, are the best. I would be delighted if one of my friends fed me a frittata with a simple salad.

If you are back late from work, make sure you've read the recipe and know what you are doing. Take note if you need to preheat the oven, as not doing this can really slow down your meal and hamper your enjoyment.

I work along the lines of classic-with-a-twist. Choose straightforward recipes during the week, and just add a cheeky twist.

Chorizo-spiked Ratatouille

Ratatouille is one of those recipes that everyone has a version of. It hails from France where it is a side dish of sautéed summer vegetables, cooked with lots of herbs. My mum's ratatouille always had marjoram thrown in at the end. Wet with red pepper and full of fresh herbs, you can serve this hot, as is traditional, or cold – the perfect accompaniment to a small roast chicken, some pitta and hummus, or just some bread and cheese.

Serves 4

3 tablespoons olive oil

1 teaspoon cumin seeds

1 yellow pepper, deseeded and roughly chopped

1 red pepper, deseeded and roughly chopped

1 orange pepper, deseeded and roughly chopped

4 garlic cloves, peeled and finely chopped

2 onions, roughly chopped

1 bay leaf

3 anchovy fillets, chopped

4 courgettes, roughly chopped

5 plum tomatoes, roughly chopped

1 x 400g can chopped tomatoes

1 heaped teaspoon caster sugar

a pinch of Maldon sea salt

freshly ground black pepper

350g hot parrilla cooking chorizo, chopped into 2.5cm pieces

a handful of mixed fresh herbs, such as parsley, oregano and marjoram

Heat the olive oil in a large saucepan over a moderate heat. When it is hot, add the cumin and peppers and cook for 10–15 minutes, stirring, until they are just beginning to brown. Turn the heat down low, add the garlic, onions, bay leaf and anchovies and sweat for 5 minutes, stirring occasionally, until the onions start to soften. Add the courgettes, fresh tomatoes and canned tomatoes, place a lid on the pan and leave to simmer for 20 minutes. Season with sugar, salt and pepper and continue to cook for a further 10 minutes with the lid off, which will allow some of the moisture to evaporate and help the ratatouille to thicken slightly. Finally, stir in the chopped chorizo and simmer for a further 5–10 minutes. Remove from the heat, leave to cool and then scatter with the ripped-up garden herbs.

 I've included chorizo in this version to add spice and bulk, but feel free to revert to the original vegetarian dish.

Puy Lentils with Goat's Cheese

Grown in the Le Puy region of France, these lentils are considered one of the best pulses. Peppery, with a firm shape, they are ordinarily served in France with deep meats – confits of duck, goose and pork. The lentils are clean and cut the fattiness of the meats. I was brought up on pulses and they really are the best way to have a simple, tasty, one-pot supper. Creamy, earthy, savoury and yet delicately sweet, I have started serving my lentils with a roundel of goat's cheese because it adds a comforting, creamy, extra tang and packs an even more French punch.

Serves 2

3 tablespoons olive oil
1 onion, finely chopped
2 carrots, finely diced
2 celery sticks, finely diced
3 garlic cloves, peeled and crushed
1 bay leaf
200g dried Puy lentils
120g cherry tomatoes
6 sprigs of fresh thyme
Maldon sea salt
freshly ground black pepper
a handful of fresh curly parsley, finely
  chopped
200g goat's cheese, such as Bûche
  de Chèvre

Heat the olive oil in a medium saucepan over a moderate heat. Add the onion, carrots and celery and allow to sweat for 5–10 minutes until the vegetables are starting to soften. Add the garlic and bay leaf and keep stirring for a further 5 minutes until the onion is translucent. Add the lentils and 1 litre water and bring to the boil. Put on a lid and simmer gently for 20 minutes until most of the water has been absorbed. Throw in the tomatoes, strip the leaves off the thyme and add them to the pan. Continue to cook for a further 10 minutes with the lid on. Only when the lentils are completely cooked can you season them. (If you season too soon the salt will prevent the pulses from softening.) Taste to check the dish is well seasoned, and then spoon the lentils into serving bowls. To serve, sprinkle with some chopped parsley and crumble over the goat's cheese. Accompany with some bread to mop up all the juices.

 If you are in need of some meat, fry off a few rashers of chopped bacon or a small saucisson and add it to the lentils at the last minute.

Cinnamon Moussaka

Moussaka is a moniker Greek dish. My grandmother's moussaka was traditionally lamby and rich, but my version is inspired by my Greek friend Kay who makes hers vegetarian rather than the meaty classic. I have used labneh on top, instead of a more traditional béchamel lid, which gives a really nice tart edge. Labneh, a rich and creamy dairy product, is a strained yogurt closer to Middle Eastern food. It marries nicely with the heavy dose of cumin and cinnamon.

Serves 4

3 large waxy potatoes, such as Maris Piper or Désirée, peeled (about 600g)
sea salt
2 large aubergines (about 600g), sliced lengthways into 5mm slices
50ml olive oil
2 large courgettes (about 500g), sliced lengthways into 5mm strips
2 x 400g cans chopped tomatoes
1 tablespoon tomato purée
1 fresh bay leaf
2 teaspoons ground cinnamon
a pinch of chilli flakes
1 teaspoon ground cumin
1 teaspoon dried oregano
1 teaspoon golden caster sugar
1 tablespoon Worcestershire sauce
500g labneh or strained Greek yogurt
3 eggs
½ teaspoon ground nutmeg
300g Cheddar (I use Longman's), grated
50g Parmesan

Place the potatoes in a pan of salted water and bring to the boil. Simmer for 20 minutes or until they are parboiled – i.e. tender, but not fully cooked. Place the aubergines in a colander, scatter over some salt to draw out the moisture and set aside for about 20 minutes, or until pearls of water appear on the surface.

Heat a few tablespoons of olive oil in a large frying pan on a high heat and fry the courgettes until they are golden on both sides. Transfer to some kitchen paper to absorb any excess oil. Rinse the aubergine under a tap to remove the salt and squeeze to further remove any moisture. Add more oil to the pan and fry the aubergines until mid-brown. Drain on some kitchen paper. Arrange the courgettes and aubergines in the base of your baking dish. Drain the potatoes, cut into 5mm thick slices and layer them up on top of the fried vegetables. Set aside.

Preheat the oven to 180°C/gas mark 4. To make the tomato sauce, place the chopped tomatoes in a medium saucepan over a moderate heat. Add the tomato purée, bay leaf, cinnamon, chilli flakes, cumin, oregano, sugar, ½ teaspoon salt and the Worcestershire sauce. Simmer until the sauce has reduced by half and is just beginning to catch on the bottom of the pan – about 15 minutes. Spoon the tomato sauce over the vegetables and bake in the oven for 30 minutes.

To make the topping, place the labneh, eggs, nutmeg and Cheddar in a bowl and beat together with a fork – it should taste slightly tart. Remove the moussaka from the oven and spread the cheesy sauce over the top. Grate over the Parmesan and return to the oven for a further 30 minutes (1 hour in total) until the moussaka is bubbling at the edges and browning and blistering on top.

Tamarind Tadka Dal with Yogurt Rice

The rice recipe here comes from my old friend Bharat. His family moved to Newcastle from India in 1972 and with them brought unheard of methods and aromas. The curry leaves are a must – their delicate scent rises from the pan as they blister and curl. When I'm eating this I search out the leaves and suck all the flavour from them like sweets. Bharat's mother Devi always used cracked basmati rice. Do try and get hold of it as it makes a real difference and lends a fine creaminess that is integral to the dish.

Serves 3–4, depending on your hunger

For the dal

250g split yellow lentils (chana dal), rinsed
80g tomatoes, sliced into quarters
1 tablespoon coconut or vegetable oil
1 green pepper, deseeded and cut into slices lengthways
1 onion, roughly sliced
2 garlic cloves, peeled and sliced
5cm piece of fresh root ginger, peeled and cut into matchsticks
3 small green chillies, finely sliced
2 dried red chillies, roughly chopped
2 teaspoons mustard seeds
2 teaspoons garam masala
1 teaspoon ground turmeric
1 teaspoon ground coriander
2 teaspoons cumin seeds
1 teaspoon sea salt
1 teaspoon caster sugar
2 tablespoons tamarind concentrate (available from Asian supermarkets)

Start with the dal as this needs a long simmer. Place the lentils in a pan with 1.2 litres water (no salt). Bring to the boil. Simmer over a low heat, with the lid tilted on top, for about 1 hour – by which time most of the liquid will have absorbed and the pulses should be soft and swollen. Keeping the pan on the heat, add the tomatoes and cook for a further 30 minutes. The lentils should now be breaking up and the dal should be thick and saucy. Remove from the heat.

Meanwhile, place the rice in a medium pan with 500ml water and a pinch of salt. Bring to the boil on a high heat, and then turn down to moderate. Simmer for 10 minutes, or until all of the water has evaporated and you are left with little bubbling funnels dotted over the rice. Turn the heat off, place a lid on the pan to retain the steam and leave to stand for half an hour. Rice is all about patience (as my husband so frequently tells me!).

To make the flavouring for the rice, heat the oil in a frying pan on a high heat. Add the red onions and let them brown slightly, tossing the pan from time to time. Now add the garlic, curry leaves, chilli, mustard seeds and cardamom. Keep tossing the pan for a few minutes to allow the seeds to pop and the scent to rise. Remove from the heat and set aside to cool slightly. When the rice has cooled to room temperature, fluff it up with a fork (always a fork and never a spoon) and turn it out into a salad bowl. Gently fold in the spiced onion mixture and then the yogurt. Season with salt and a little pepper to taste.

For the rice

250g cracked basmati rice (available from Asian supermarkets)

pinch of salt

2 tablespoons coconut or vegetable oil

2 red onions, roughly sliced

3 garlic cloves, peeled and finely chopped

a generous handful of really fresh curry leaves (available from Asian supermarkets)

1 green chilli, finely chopped

3 teaspoons brown mustard seeds

8 whole green cardamom pods

220g strained Greek yogurt

salt and black pepper, to taste

To complete the dal, heat the oil over a high heat in a small frying pan or tadka pan. In quick succession, throw in the pepper and onion. Toss quickly to coat the vegetables in the oil and then fry for a few minutes until starting to brown. Add the garlic, ginger and chillies and toss well again. Add the mustard seeds, garam masala, turmeric, coriander and cumin and stir so that the spices release their fragrance. Turn the heat down slightly to stop the spices from scorching and cook for a couple of minutes. To serve, season the dal with salt, sugar and tamarind concentrate, and then tip the spicy, sizzling tadka over the top. Swirl together to combine and serve with the rice on the side.

When making the dal, it is most important to quickly fry your spices in a tadka and add to your pulses at the very last moment.

Baked Meatballs with Creamed Basil and Parmesan Spinach

When I was little meatballs came in my mum's delicious tomatoey sauce and were served with spaghetti, Italian-American style. In this recipe I've taken them on a different journey, making them with rye instead of regular breadcrumbs and flavouring them with dill seeds – an ingredient I can't get enough of. This gives the meatballs a slightly Scandinavian flavour, far away from the traditional tomato sauce. You want to use really good homegrown (big) spinach for the accompaniment – check out your local farmers' market instead of going to the supermarket as the shop-bought stuff tends to be a bit babyish.

Serves 4

For the meatballs (makes 12–16 balls)
500g minced pork
1 onion, grated
1 small courgette, grated
30g rye crackers, ground into breadcrumbs
1 teaspoon dill seeds
1 large egg, beaten
½ teaspoon sea salt
freshly ground black pepper
60ml vegetable oil
150ml vegetable stock

For the creamed spinach
750g big-leaved fresh spinach, washed
100g butter
50g plain flour
300ml vegetable stock
50ml white wine
50ml whole milk
20g fresh basil, finely chopped
30g Parmesan, finely grated
sea salt
freshly ground black pepper

Place the pork in a mixing bowl with the grated onion and courgette. Give this a really good mash with your fists. Mix the ground rye crackers into the pork, along with the dill seeds, the beaten egg and some seasoning. Combine really well with your hands so that all of the ingredients are evenly distributed.

Preheat the oven to 180°C/gas mark 4. Fashion the mixture into balls in your palms, flatten them slightly and place on a plate ready for browning. Heat the vegetable oil in a wide frying pan over a moderate heat until it is really hot. Turn down the temperature slightly and add the meatballs a few at a time. Fry in batches until golden on both sides, about 2–4 minutes, then transfer to a baking dish with a slotted spoon. Pour over the stock so that it comes halfway up the sides of the meatballs. Cover with foil and bake in the oven for 45 minutes.

Place the spinach leaves in a large pan on a low heat and fit a lid. Steam the spinach until it has halved in size and remove to a sieve. To make the béchamel, heat the butter on a low heat in a medium saucepan. When it has melted entirely, add the plain flour. Using a whisk, beat to combine and cook out the flour for a couple of minutes. Gradually pour in the vegetable stock, whisking all the time to avoid lumps. Then add the white wine and milk, whisking continuously. Bring to the boil and simmer for 2 minutes. Meanwhile, squeeze out the water from the spinach and chop finely. Add to the sauce with the basil, Parmesan and seasoning. Serve the meatballs with the creamed spinach on the side and some plain new potatoes.

Pepperoncini Frittata

I learnt this trick for cooking peppers from my Italian friend Ileana. Fried then poached in a little stock, the strips of pepper become soft and almost jammy. Utilise this method for the ultimate frittata, or simply cook up the peppers and serve as a salad with lemon juice and garlic. This recipe is just one way of making a frittata. You can add pretty much anything – spring onions, tomatoes, Parmesan, spinach, bacon – so just use what you have available – perfect for a weeknight supper.

Makes 4 thick wedges

4 tablespoons olive oil

2 red peppers, deseeded and sliced into strips

200ml vegetable stock

1 small onion, finely sliced

4 free-range eggs

70g goat's cheese

a handful of parsley, basil or marjoram, finely chopped

lots of freshly ground black pepper

a little sea salt

For a cracking omelette, first combine your chosen ingredients with the eggs and thoroughly beat together, and then pour the whole lot into your pan. Your omelette will hold together every time.

Heat half of the oil in a medium frying pan over a moderate heat. When it is quivering, add the peppers and sauté for a few minutes to coat them in the oil. Pour in the vegetable stock and simmer for about 20 minutes until it has all evaporated – this will ensure the peppers are evenly cooked and make them really tender. When there is no liquid left and all you have is the original oil, turn up the heat and continue frying the peppers until they are flecked with brown and give off a charcoal scent. Remove the peppers from the pan with a slotted spoon and place on a plate to cool. Return the pan to a moderate heat, add the onion and fry until soft and translucent – about 5 minutes. You may need to add a little extra olive oil if things are sticking. Transfer to the plate with the peppers.

Heat the remaining olive oil in a cast-iron frying pan on a medium-to-high heat. Whilst this gets hot, beat the eggs in a measuring jug and stir in the cooked peppers and onions. Crumble in the goat's cheese, add the parsley and seasoning and combine really well with a fork. Once it is evenly mixed, pour the whole lot into the pan and give it a quick shake to settle the frittata. Turn the heat to low and leave to cook for 5 minutes, or until the frittata is starting to firm up around the edges but is still wobbly in the centre. Preheat your grill to medium. To finish, crisp up your frittata under the grill and cook until it is just turning golden brown. Leave to stand for 5 minutes in the pan before turning out onto a plate.

Potato Cakes with Smoked Haddock and a Pickled Cucumber Salad

Potato cakes are one of my dad's staple snacks. This is mostly due to his stern and Edwardian dislike of waste. You can always do something with a little leftover mashed or boiled potato. Or if you don't have leftover potatoes, then it is easy to boil up a batch for this recipe. I have used polenta, which gives a far superior crust to the usual breadcrumb coating here too. The pickled cucumber salad is a must as it brings the whole meal zinging to life and is incredibly easy to prepare.

Serves 3

1 cucumber, peeled and finely sliced

200ml white balsamic vinegar (or white wine vinegar)

1 red chilli, sliced in half

60g golden caster sugar

2 teaspoons mustard seeds

a pinch of sea salt

450g floury potatoes, such as Désirée, peeled or 450g leftover mashed potato

450g skinless smoked haddock

150ml whole milk

1 bay leaf, crushed

½ teaspoon fenugreek seeds

a pinch of sea salt

lots of freshly ground black pepper

zest of ½ lemon

1 egg, beaten

150g fine polenta

100ml vegetable oil

It may seem like I have stipulated quite a lot of oil for frying but you want to shallow-fry these for the ultimate crispy shell and creamy insides.

First make the salad. Lay the sliced cucumber in a shallow dish. Combine the vinegar, chilli, sugar, mustard seeds and salt in a small saucepan. Place on a high heat until the sugar has dissolved and the vinegar has reduced by one-third. Pour immediately over the cucumber and set aside to infuse for a couple of hours. When you are ready to serve, drain off most of the pickle, leaving just enough to coat.

To make the potato cakes, place the potatoes in a pan of water on a high heat and boil until soft. Drain thoroughly and roughly mash with a fork. Set aside. Meanwhile, place the haddock in a wide frying pan and pour over the milk. Add the crushed bay leaf and fenugreek seeds. Place the pan on a low heat and simmer gently for about 5 minutes until the fish is just cooked and beginning to flake. Using a slotted spoon, remove the fish to a plate and leave to cool. To make the fishcakes, combine the cooled potato with the haddock in a bowl. Season and add the lemon zest and egg and combine thoroughly.

Scatter the polenta onto a plate ready for coating the fishcakes and have another clean plate to hand. Shape the mixture into 9 cakes with your hands, roll in the polenta and then transfer them to the clean plate. Heat the oil in a large, wide frying pan over a high heat. When it is quivering hot, turn down the heat to medium and gently place the cakes in the pan. You may need to cook them in batches. Fry until they are crisp and golden on the first side before turning them over and cooking them on the other side. Drain on kitchen paper to absorb any excess oil and serve with the cucumber salad.

Cheesy Potato Cakes with Garlic Dressed Dwarf Beans

This recipe shows how easy it is to vary potato cakes. The ingredients are what I felt like using at the time, which is the whole point of potato cakes. You can include a little of whatever you fancy – finely sliced leeks, a handful of bruised basil, some crushed anchovies, or leftover peas. It is up to your fridge to decide. This version calls for sun-dried tomatoes and capers, but you can use just one of these ingredients, and even throw in a few sliced black olives if you have them.

Serves 3–4

900g floury potatoes, such as Désirée, peeled

80g Lancashire cheese (I use Mrs Kirkham's)

90g sun-dried tomatoes

1 heaped tablespoon capers

a small handful of finely chopped parsley

1 beaten egg

lots of sea salt

lots of freshly ground black pepper

150g polenta

400g dwarf beans

3–4 garlic cloves

1 tablespoon white balsamic vinegar

3 tablespoons extra virgin olive oil

100ml vegetable oil

Boil your potatoes until they are really soft. Drain, mash and cool. When the potatoes are at room temperature, grate in the cheese. Finely chop the sun-dried tomatoes and add them to the bowl along with the capers and chopped parsley. Give everything a thorough mix and then stir in the beaten egg (this will glue your cakes together). Season generously. Measure out the polenta onto a plate. Divide the mixture into 9 potato cakes, shape into patties in the palms of your hands and roll in the polenta. Place on a plate, cover with clingfilm and set aside in the fridge to firm up for about 1 hour.

To make the salad, trim the dwarf beans, place in a saucepan and cover with water. Bring to the boil and cook for 5 minutes, or until the beans are al dente. (If your beans are slightly woody, you might prefer to cook them a bit longer until they become tender.) Drain and place in a wide salad bowl. Crush the garlic and combine with the vinegar and olive oil to make a dressing. Pour over the green beans whilst they are still warm.

To cook the potato cakes, heat the vegetable oil in a large frying pan on a high heat. When the oil is shimmering but not smoking hot, turn the heat to medium and add the potato cakes. Fry until crisp and golden on both sides – this will only take a few minutes. Remove from the pan, drain on kitchen paper to mop up any excess oil and serve immediately with your dressed beans.

Lemon and Dill Baked Grey Mullet

This recipe couldn't be simpler. I love baking fish in foil as it's so easy. It is all in the preparation of clean flavours. What is so brilliant about this method is that in steaming the fish in the foil, the flavours you have employed infuse the entirety. You can play around with your ingredients too: basil and orange? Chervil and garlic butter? Parsley and cherry tomatoes? Ginger, chilli and soy? Try it with the Chive Flower Potato Salad on page 56 and some freshly dressed leaves.

Serves 4

2 lemons, sliced into discs
1kg grey mullet, scaled and gutted
40g fresh dill
2 tablespoons extra virgin olive oil
sea salt
freshly ground pepper
1 lemon, cut into wedges, to serve

Preheat the oven to 200°C/gas mark 6. Prepare a large baking tray by lining with foil double its size. Place a line of lemon slices diagonally across the foil. Rest the grey mullet over these. Open up the stomach cavity and stuff with the complete fronds of dill. Wedge some more lemon slices in here too. Layer more slices of lemon over the top of the fish, drizzle over the olive oil and season generously. Fold over the excess foil and seal the edges so that you have a foil pillow. No air should be able to escape. Place in the oven for 20–30 minutes. Remove and let it sit and cool for 15 minutes. Serve with some of the baked wilted dill and some fresh wedges of lemon.

Warm Whole Roasted Beet Salad

In England it has always been popular to pickle beetroot. However, roasted, the beetroots take on a delicious sweetness but retain their hearty, meaty texture too. I made this brilliant, bright salad for my friend Alice's birthday party. Over the years we've hatched a lot of meals and danced at a lot of parties together. Since then it's become a real staple dish for us and it always reminds me of that really great party with our friends going back to the table again and again for more sustenance.

Serves 3–4

4 large fresh beetroots, complete with
    tops
3 large carrots
2 tablespoons olive oil
2 handfuls of baby spinach leaves
100g hazelnuts
100g fresh, soft ricotta cheese
1 tablespoon balsamic vinegar

Preheat the oven to 180°C/gas mark 4. Wash the beetroots thoroughly and remove the tops, setting them aside. Chop the beetroots into 6 pieces each and the carrots into 8. Place on a baking tray, pour over the oil and put in the oven for 1 hour until tender and golden brown.

Meanwhile, roughly chop the beetroot tops and place in a big salad bowl with the spinach leaves. Heat a dry frying pan and toss the nuts so that they toast just a little. Remove to cool on a plate (or they will continue to toast, and burn).

When the vegetables are ready, pile onto the leaves with the excess oil. Crumble over the ricotta followed by the nuts, and dress with a little vinegar. Serve with crusty bread.

 This is a brilliant salad to make for loads of friends because it's really easy to double and triple the quantities without having to be too precise.

Salt and Pepper Squid with Dipping Sauce

Salt and pepper squid is a favourite out-for-dinner choice. I can't resist this crisp and yet soft delight. To make it at home, all you need is some nice squid and a generous heaping of Szechuan peppercorns. Once I mastered this dish it became a regular treat. Make a dipping sauce and you will feel like you're out at a slap-up restaurant.

Serves 2

For the dipping sauce
100ml rice vinegar
3 bird's eye chillies, finely chopped
1 tablespoon caster sugar
1 teaspoon fish sauce
4cm piece of cucumber

For the squid
650g squid, cleaned with the bone removed
2 teaspoons Szechuan peppercorns
½ teaspoon coarse sea salt
80g plain flour
550ml vegetable oil

Measure out the vinegar into a small saucepan. Add the chillies, sugar and fish sauce and bring this to a gentle boil. Simmer for a few minutes and then turn off the heat. Decant to a ramekin to cool. Meanwhile, peel the cucumber and deseed. Slice this into matchstick size strips and then dice into tiny pieces. Add these to the dipping sauce and set aside.

Ask your fishmonger to clean and remove the bone of the squid, but make sure to hold onto the tentacles (these go wonderfully crisp when fried). Slice the main squid into strips about 2cm wide. Score the flesh so that you have a lattice design. Set these aside with the tentacles. In a pestle and mortar, grind the Szechuan peppercorns with the salt so that you have a rough spice mix. Measure the flour onto a large plate and mix with this the salt and pepper. Now, grab your moist squid pieces and toss them in the flour mix.

Heat the oil in a medium pan over a high heat. When it is piping hot and visibly moving in the pan add the battered squid in batches. Let it fizz and fry and become a little golden and then transfer with a slotted spoon to some kitchen paper. Continue until you have fried all of your fish. Serve immediately with the dipping sauce and a fresh lime Thai salad if you wish.

Orzo Yellow Tomato Salad

This is a slightly more sophisticated take on the staple pasta salad, using orzo pasta, which is deceptively rice-shaped. The tomatoes, onion and herbs make for a riotous bowl of colour. We serve this dish in the deli during the summer when customers are craving something sharp and refreshing. Add some pitted black olives and capers to go the extra mile.

Serves 4

For the salad

160g orzo pasta
500g yellow baby plum tomatoes (or red if you can't find these)
1 medium red onion, finely diced
30g curly parsley, finely chopped
a few sprigs of lemon thyme, shredded
20g basil, finely chopped

For the dressing

1 tablespoon white wine vinegar
3 tablespoons extra virgin olive oil
3 garlic cloves, crushed
1 teaspoon caster sugar
½ teaspoon sea salt
freshly ground pepper

Bring a pan of salted water to the boil. Add the orzo pasta and simmer until it is well cooked – a little more than al dente (check the packet instructions as they vary). Drain the pasta and rinse under cold water to cool.

Meanwhile, wash the tomatoes and halve if they are small and quarter if they are bigger. Place these in a deep salad bowl with the red onion and parsley, lemon thyme and basil. Add the cooled pasta and give this a good toss with your hands.

To make the dressing, find a jar with a matching lid. Add the vinegar, extra virgin olive oil, garlic cloves, sugar, salt and pepper. Place the lid on the jar and give it a mixologist's shake. Pour the dressing over the salad and thoroughly mix through. Let the salad sit for a few hours to really infuse before serving.

 In winter, you can also add orzo to soups and stews to thicken them and inject some much-needed carbs.

Sardines Escabeche

I love everything pickled – roll mops, anchovies, capers, it's all good – and these Sardines Escabeche are a classic old-school way of doing just that. The original recipe came from one of the Moro books to which I turn regularly for inspiration. These little fish have gone down really well at the supper clubs that we do at the café. The most important thing is that you get good sardines. They are a very inexpensive fish, so it is worth forking out a few more pennies for some really fresh juicy finds. This recipe uses gram flour as that is what I had to hand.

Serves 3

3 tablespoons gram flour

1 teaspoon ground turmeric

6 sardines, weighing about 800kg, gutted and scaled

3 tablespoons olive oil

80ml red wine vinegar

1 fresh bay leaf

a few sprigs of dried thyme, on the stalk

1 teaspoon green peppercorns

1 big dried chilli

1 teaspoon fennel seeds

1 head of dill flowers (off my gone-to-seed-dill plant)

a generous pinch of salt

a generous pinch of sugar

½ red pepper, very finely sliced

½ onion, very finely sliced

2 teaspoons capers in vinegar

On a large plate, mix together the flour and turmeric. Pat the sardines dry and then dust in the flour. Heat the olive oil in a large pan and then fry the fishes until they are golden and a little crisp. This will be about 1 minute on each side. Transfer with a fish slice to a shallow serving dish.

Using the same pan, place on a medium heat and add the vinegar, and then in close succession, the bay leaf, thyme, peppercorns, chilli, fennel seeds, dill, salt and sugar. It will simmer and the delicious sharp flavours should slightly catch the back of your throat. Now add the pepper and onion and simmer for a few minutes to soften, but not totally cook. Immediately, pour the mix over the sardines, and then scatter over the capers. Leave this to sit for a few hours before serving. It's good to note that in the original recipe Sam and Sam Clark recommend leaving this for the flavours to develop for up to 48 hours. I'm usually too hungry though, so haven't got the patience for that!

If your fishmonger has not gutted or cleaned the sardines, you will need to do so: slice down the belly of the fish and gently remove their innards with your thumb. Once you get over the initial ickiness, this is actually fine. Slice off their heads and wash under a running tap.

Schnitzel with Lemon Thyme Mash

When my grandmother, Bunty, was a young mother, she took workers in on her farm. One couple, refugees from Austria and Yugoslavia, taught her to make this traditional Austrian dish. Originally it was made with veal but Bunty makes hers with slivers of pork. Whenever I stayed with Bunty as a child we would play cards and she would make this for our supper. As she tucked me into bed at night we would say our prayers together and I would feel like the safest and most guarded little girl around.

Serves 2

For the mash
400g potatoes, such as King Edward,
    peeled and halved
40g butter
50ml whole milk
freshly ground black pepper
sea salt
a few sprigs of lemon thyme

For the schnitzel
2 x 150g thin pork leg steaks
3 tablespoons plain flour
50g fresh or dried breadcrumbs
1 egg, beaten
½ teaspoon sea salt
freshly ground black pepper
3 tablespoons vegetable oil

To serve
1 tablespoon capers
1 lemon, cut into wedges

Start the mash first. Place the potatoes in a large pan of salted water. Bring to the boil and simmer for about 30 minutes. When the potatoes fall off a sharp knife easily they are ready. Drain and return the potatoes to the pan. Add the butter and milk and mash thoroughly until it is creamy and light. Season generously with pepper, salt and the shredded lemon thyme. Place a lid on the mash while you make the schnitzel.

Sandwich each steak between clingfilm and then, on a sturdy worktop, beat each one with a rolling pin until it is about 5mm thick.

Get yourself ready for coating the steaks by measuring the flour onto one plate, the breadcrumbs onto another, and beating the egg into a large bowl. First dust each of the steaks all over in flour. Dip in the egg, and then coat in the breadcrumbs so they are entirely coated on both sides. Season thoroughly.

Heat the oil in a wide frying pan on a high heat. Check to see if the oil is hot enough by adding a pinch of breadcrumbs – they should dance in the pan. Add the schnitzels and cook for about 3 minutes on each side until golden brown. Remove from the pan straight away onto serving plates, scatter with the capers and accompany with lemon wedges.

 It is important to drench the schnitzel in lemon so that the crisp breaded shell becomes soft and crumbly again. Perfection!

Instant Mulberry Chutney with Crottin and Hazelnuts

This chutney is an uncharacteristic quickie. Done in small amounts, when you have
a hankering for vinegar and sugar and fruit, but haven't forward-planned. It was
with huge intrigue and excitement that I first discovered white dried mulberries in
one of my favourite Iranian shops. They eat them like sweets in the Nour, but these
mulberries also lend themselves to tart sauces and work well in salads and mueslis. So
I have included these Iranian sweets in my instant chutney, to bring a sort of Middle
Eastern influence.

Serves 4

For the chutney

2 red onions, finely sliced
2 teaspoons caraway seeds
250g dried white mulberries
500ml white Italian vinegar
200g dark muscovado sugar
sea salt

To serve

a generous handful of peeled, halved
    hazelnuts
a few handfuls of fresh salad leaves
a little extra virgin olive oil
4 small, fresh Crottin goat's cheeses

Place the onions, caraway seeds, mulberries and vinegar in
a saucepan over a moderate heat. Bring to the boil and then
simmer until the onions are slippery soft and the mulberries are
swollen and fat – about 10 minutes. Add the sugar, stir well to
dissolve, and then simmer for a further 10 minutes until the
chutney has thickened and deepened in colour. Season with a
little salt if necessary, and then cool to room temperature.

Toast the hazelnuts in a dry frying pan over a low heat. When
they start to turn golden in parts, tip them onto a plate and
cool to room temperature. (If you leave them in the pan they
will continue to cook and might burn.)

To serve, dress the salad leaves with a little olive oil and arrange
on a plate with the goat's cheeses and hazelnuts. Spoon over
some of the white mulberry chutney.

This is the sort of thing you can whip up in an instant if someone
brings over some good cheese. It is best served with the freshest
little Crottin goat's cheeses, toasted nuts and salad.

Sweet Potato and Fennel Gratin

Gratin is a classic French dish of shallow-baked creamy potatoes with a cheesy lid. Failing to find any nice potatoes on the market last year, I started making it with sweet potatoes, which have a much more fluffy and soft texture than our firmer and waxy British potato, especially when baked. My gratin is inspired by my mum's more classic version, which hails from France, where thyme is a frequent addition to many recipes. Thyme is also commonly used in Jamaica: so by adding thyme to the sweet potato gratin you are both honouring the original recipe and a new one, making a perfect crossover.

Serves 2

1kg sweet potatoes (the ones with pinky
  orange flesh)
500g whole fennel
2 tablespoons olive oil
Maldon sea salt
freshly ground black pepper
100g unsalted butter
a few sprigs of fresh thyme
284ml double cream
120g Gruyère or Comté

Preheat the oven to 180°C/gas mark 4. Place the sweet potatoes in a sink of warm water and give them a good scrub. Peel under a running tap, removing all the gnarly bits, and finely slice. I use a food-processor to finely slice them, but if you haven't got one a mandolin or some accurate slicing works fine. Place the potato discs in a large bowl. Trim and finely slice the fennel bulbs and add to the bowl. Drizzle over the oil, season generously and toss everything together to coat. Layer the vegetables in your baking dish, scatter over some knobs of butter and sprinkle with the thyme leaves. Pour over the double cream and bake in the oven for 40 minutes, or until the gratin has sunk down slightly and is blistering a little on top. Grate over the cheese and finish off under the grill until blistered and brown on top.

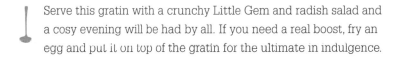

Serve this gratin with a crunchy Little Gem and radish salad and a cosy evening will be had by all. If you need a real boost, fry an egg and put it on top of the gratin for the ultimate in indulgence.

Hummus with Ground Lamb

Hummus has always been a constant in my life. Given my mum's love of pulses it was a natural regular on the menu at home. And in keeping with my childhood, we make it daily at Rosie's. The key to a good hummus is in zooping it up. A lot. Don't hold back on any of it – the garlic, the lemon juice and the tahini. This hummus recipe goes the extra mile. Just by sweating a little ground lamb and adding some golden pine nuts and pomegranate, you will turn the ordinary into the brilliant.

Serves 4–6

For the hummus

450g cooked chickpeas, drained

3 garlic cloves, peeled and chopped

juice of 1–1½ lemons

1 heaped tablespoon tahini

½ teaspoon sea salt

2 tablespoons extra virgin olive oil

For the ground lamb

2 tablespoons olive oil

1 small onion, finely diced

1 teaspoon ground cumin

½ teaspoon ground cinnamon

½ teaspoon paprika

250g minced lamb

1 teaspoon tomato purée

½ teaspoon sea salt

30g pine nuts, toasted

½ pomegranate, seeds beaten out

Place all the hummus ingredients in a deep jug or bowl. Using a handheld blender, work until it is really smooth. This may take a little elbow grease. Taste to make sure that is it punchy and bursting with flavour. Add more of any of the ingredients if you feel it is at all lacking and, if it is proving hard to blend, add a little water to loosen. Spread the hummus into a medium bowl with quite high sides, making a well in the middle. Set this aside.

To make the ground lamb, heat the olive oil in a large pan over a medium heat. Add the onion and sweat for a few minutes before adding the cumin, cinnamon and paprika. Mix and fry the spices. Now add the lamb. Using a heatproof spatula, thoroughly work the mince to break it up. You are aiming for something very fine. Now mix in the tomato purée and salt. Continue to heat over a low heat for a few minutes before removing from the heat. Let this cool for 10 minutes and then tip this into the well in the hummus. Scatter over the pine nuts and pomegranate seeds and serve up with grilled pitta breads.

Larb (Thai Salad)

I was always unsure of Larb. The idea of a salad with minced meat seemed too odd to me. But that was until I tried it at our local Thai restaurant. Here they make their larb hot hot hot and wet and moreish and grainy. It is a life-changing salad. And, as if by magic, I have recently become friends with a lovely Thai lady called Nok. She has been telling me all sorts of Bangkok secrets but most notably the trick with Larb. It is all in the roasting of the rice. This gives that particularly nutty bite to the dish and cannot be circumnavigated.

Serves 6 as a starter or 4 as a main course

For the dressing
1 dried red chilli
3 discs of galangal
1 lemongrass stick
3 garlic cloves, finely chopped
1 tablespoon caster sugar
3 fresh bird's eye chillies, finely chopped
3 limes
1 tablespoon Thai fish sauce

For the salad
30g sticky rice
1 large red onion, finely sliced
½ iceberg lettuce, half shredded, half broken
10g mint, torn
10g Thai basil, torn
1 tablespoon vegetable oil
400g minced pork or chicken

First make the dressing. Place the dried chilli and galangal discs in a dry frying pan and toast on a medium heat until they are charred and crisp. Place these in a pestle and mortar. Remove the outer woody sheath from the lemongrass and finely slice the inner, softer core. Place this in the pestle and add the garlic, sugar and fresh chillies. Give this a good grind and then add the juice of one of the limes. Give it another thorough grind and then add the rest of the lime juice and fish sauce. Set this aside so that the sugar can fully dissolve and the flavours merge.

For the ground rice, place the sticky rice in a dry frying pan and toast on a moderate heat until the grains are becoming yellow and jiggle in the pan. Keep tossing to prevent burning. When the rice is ready, remove to a pestle and mortar and grind to a fine sand-like texture. Set this aside.

In a salad bowl, mix together the red onion, lettuce leaves, mint and basil. Heat the vegetable oil in a large frying pan and add the minced pork or chicken. Work over this carefully so that you gradually get a totally broken up cooked mass. It should look like bolognese mince (I use a heatproof spatula which works wonderfully). Remove the pan from the heat and let it sit for few moments before tipping the pork over the salad. Pour over the dressing and scatter over the previously prepared ground rice.

Grilled Mackerel with Pomelo Salad

Mackerel has long been paired with tart fruit accompaniments. It serves to cut the rich, dense, oily nature of one of my favourite fishes. This combination came to me like a thief in the night. I'd already made the pomelo salad many times – a recipe that I nabbed off my friends Kylie and Bharat, who have a great collection of Asian recipes. It's a really refreshing salad made with a fruit that looks a bit like a grapefruit, though not as tart. It's fresh and light and lends itself really well to chilli. So it seemed like the next logical step was to combine the pomelo salad with mackerel and see what happened. Drink with a cold beer. This is brilliantly HOT.

Serves 2

For the salad
1 whole pomelo
2 fresh red bird's eye chillies, finely
    chopped
a handful of garlic chives, roughly
    chopped
a handful of beansprouts
3 spring onions, sliced into shards
a handful of unsalted peanuts
1 teaspoon fish sauce
juice of 2 limes
1 tablespoon palm sugar (available from
    good Asian supermarkets)
1 tablespoon fried shallots (available in
    tubs from Chinese supermarkets)
a handful of fresh mint, roughly chopped

For the mackerel
4 mackerel fillets
dark soy sauce

First prepare the salad. Peel the pomelo, removing as much pith as you can. Slice into segments, releasing the flesh and leaving behind the tough pulp. Place the segments in a serving bowl. Add the chillies, garlic chives, beansprouts and spring onions and mix gently together. Using a pestle and mortar, roughly break up the peanuts and scatter over the salad.

To make the dressing, combine the fish sauce, lime juice and palm sugar in your pestle and mortar and mix until smooth. Pour over the salad, sprinkle with the shallots and mint and set aside to allow the flavours to infuse whilst you cook the mackerel.

Preheat the grill to high. Place the mackerel fillets, flesh-side-up, on a board. Using a pastry brush, brush the flesh all over with dark soy sauce so that it seeps in. It is deep and strong, so don't overload the fish. Place the mackerel, skin-side up, on a grill tray and set under the grill for 4 minutes, or until the skin is crisp. Now turn the fillets over and grill for a further minute on the other side until the flesh is just cooked and tender. Serve with the pomelo salad on the side.

It is worth investing in some deep-fried shallots. They come in handy for many Asian dishes, giving a sweet grainy crunch.

Gnocchi with a Spicy Sausage Sauce and Hazelnuts

Gnocchi, one of my grandmother's favourites, is a sensory treat – both moist and ever
so slightly springy, fleshy and yet absorbent. It works well with less sauce rather than
more, or even just a flavoured butter for coating. Prevalent across Italy, each region
has its own variation of this potato pasta. The sauce here is inspired by a dish I ate
in an Italian restaurant where I found the combination of olive-oil-heavy tomatoes
with woody, crunchy hazelnuts a brilliant revelation. Gnocchi calls for starchy, fluffy
potatoes and try to keep the dough warm to prevent a resultant chewy dumpling (a
mistake I have made before).

Serves 3

For the sauce
500g baby plum tomatoes
3 tablespoons olive oil
1 medium onion, finely chopped
1 large fresh mild chilli, finely chopped
2 teaspoons chilli flakes
200g sausagemeat
2 garlic cloves, peeled and crushed
sea salt
freshly ground black pepper
sugar, to taste

For the gnocchi
750g washed floury potatoes, such as
    Désirée
1 teaspoon sea salt
250g plain flour (preferably '00' flour), plus
    extra for dusting
1 large egg, beaten

100g whole peeled hazelnuts, toasted in a
    dry frying pan until golden
a couple of handfuls of rocket
finely grated Parmesan

Start by making the sauce. Whizz the tomatoes in a food-processor (or extensively crush them with a potato masher). Place in a medium saucepan over a moderate heat and bring to the boil. Simmer for 15 minutes until the tomatoes are reduced and thick like passata. Set aside. Heat the olive oil in a clean, medium pan over a moderate heat, add the onion, fresh chilli and chilli flakes and leave to sweat for 5 minutes until the onions are beginning to turn transparent. Add the sausagemeat and garlic and fry together for 5 minutes, breaking up the meat with a wooden spoon so that it resembles a fine ragù. When the meat is just cooked, remove from the heat and season to taste with salt, pepper and sugar and set aside.

To make the gnocchi, place the potatoes in a large pan. Cover with water and bring to the boil over a high heat. Turn the heat to medium and leave to simmer for 30–45 minutes until they are well cooked and slip really easily off a sharp knife. Drain and peel – I do this when they are still hot wearing rubber gloves – making sure there is no skin in sight. Pass the potatoes through a sieve or ricer into a clean bowl and season with salt. Measure the flour into a separate bowl. Tip the potatoes out onto a clean worksurface and make a well in the centre. Crack the egg into the well and add two-thirds of the flour. Gradually draw the flour and potatoes together until you have a dough-like ball. Knead slightly, adding the rest of the flour only if you feel it needs it – this will depend on the wetness of your potatoes. The finished dough should be moist, but not sticky.

Dust your worksurface with flour. Divide the potato dough into 6 balls and work them individually into long sausages, 2cm in diameter. Slice into thumb-knuckle-sized pieces and then roll each one along the back of a fork. Bring a large pan of salted water to the boil. When it is rumbling, add the gnocchi a couple of handfuls at a time. The gnocchi will let you know when they are cooked because they will rise up to the surface. As they do so, remove them with a slotted spoon straight into the sauce. If the sauce is too dry, you can loosen it up slightly with a couple of spoonfuls of the gnocchi water.

Serve with toasted hazelnuts, a nest of rocket and some finely grated Parmesan.

Mackerel-loaded Baked Potatoes with Sunflower Seed Salad

My mum's signature Sunday night supper has always been a baked potato, a mackerel fillet and a bursting salad. She was toasting nuts and seeds long before everyone else caught on to 'superfoods'. No salad was complete unless it included some golden sunflower seeds and big, dark pumpkin seeds scattered through it. Here I have spiced up the humble baked potato, so you feel like you are having a proper meal, but with none of the resultant fuss. Inspired by my mum's combination of flavours I've adapted her version by loading the potatoes with mackerel, so all the unctuous flavour from the fish seeps into the flesh of the potato.

Serves 2

For the potatoes

2 large baking potatoes
a few sprigs of fresh thyme
30g butter
2 spring onions, finely sliced
100g firm, mild goat's cheese
200g smoked mackerel fillets, skinned

For the salad

25g pumpkin seeds
25g sunflower seeds
2 tablespoons extra virgin olive oil
½ tablespoon pumpkin seed oil
1 tablespoon white wine vinegar
1 garlic clove
sea salt
1 large Red Gem lettuce

Preheat the oven to 200°C/gas mark 6. Place the potatoes in the oven and bake for 1 hour. Meanwhile, strip the thyme leaves into a bowl and mix together with the butter and spring onions. Grate in most of the goat's cheese and crumble in the mackerel fillets too. It should be a chunky affair. When the potatoes are ready they should be crispy and firm to the touch. Remove them from the oven and slice in half. Scoop out most of the potato flesh into the bowl with the mackerel mixture and combine well with a fork. Pile the mixture back into the potato shells, grate over the remaining cheese and place on a baking tray. Return the potatoes to the oven for a further 15 minutes. If the tops are not browning you may want to put them under the grill for a quick blast.

To prepare the salad, measure out the seeds into a dry frying pan. Toast over a low heat, tossing frequently until they are golden and popping. Tip immediately onto a plate to cool – don't leave them in the pan or they will continue to toast and may burn. In a salad bowl mix together the olive oil, pumpkin seed oil and vinegar. Finely chop the garlic on a wooden board and add a pinch of salt. Using the side of a knife, press and scrape the garlic and salt together to make a paste. Mix this in with the oils and vinegar to finish the dressing. To serve, break the lettuce leaves in half and add them to the dressing. Sprinkle in the cooled seeds and toss together. Serve the salad with the filled baked potatoes on the side.

Poppy Seed Slaw

My friend Sarah Young and I have done a lot of cooking together, both in France and in England, and I think we make a happy kitchen team. Last year we clubbed together to make a summer picnic at the Horniman Museum Gardens. Sarah's Poppy Seed Slaw was a great addition, not just visually peppering the salad, but also adding minute crackling bursts to each mouthful.

Serves 6 as part of a
big lunch

¼ white cabbage, finely sliced
½ fennel bulb, finely sliced
500g carrots, peeled and shredded
1 large red onion, finely sliced
110g natural yogurt
100g mayonnaise
juice of ½ lemon
sea salt
10g poppy seeds

This is all in the preparation and then the assembly will be easy. Place the cabbage, fennel and carrots in a large salad bowl and mix in the sliced red onion. In a measuring jug, beat together the yogurt, mayonnaise and lemon juice with a fork. Add a little sea salt and most of the poppy seeds. Pour the dressing over the slaw and give everything a really good work through with your hands to coat the salad. Sprinkle the remaining poppy seeds over the top. This salad is best left for an hour or so before eating to allow the vegetables to soften slightly.

Make sure you slice the cabbage and fennel really finely for this. I use the fine blades of a mandolin slicer to shred the carrots, but you could use a food-processor if you have one. Failing the right equipment, simply grate them on the coarse side of a grater.

Tomato Butterbeans with Fennel and Dill

Pulses are the answer to feeding on the cheap (my family mantra). If you've got some canned beans in the cupboard, you can always whip up something at the last minute. I've learnt from my parents how to make them really delicious – it usually involves adding tart tomatoes and lots of pungent herbs and spices, which is what I've done here. We make this dish a lot in the café during the grim winter months. At that time of year it seems that everyone really enjoys having a bowl of something warm, filling and a little comforting for lunch with some mopping bread on the side.

Serves 6

4 x 400g cans butterbeans in brine
3 tablespoons olive oil
1 onion, finely sliced
½ teaspoon cumin seeds
1 teaspoon fennel seeds
½ teaspoon Spanish hot smoked paprika
2 garlic cloves, peeled and finely sliced
2 celery sticks, diced
2 carrots, diced
1 whole fennel bulb, diced
3 x 400g cans chopped tomatoes
Maldon sea salt
freshly ground black pepper
1 teaspoon sugar
25g fresh dill, roughly chopped

Drain the butterbeans in a colander and rinse thoroughly. Set these aside. Heat the olive oil in a large pan over a moderate heat. When it is hot, add the onion and sweat for 5 minutes until it is translucent. Add the cumin seeds, fennel seeds and paprika and allow them to release their aroma for a few moments. In quick succession, add the garlic, celery, carrots and fennel. Give everything a good stir to coat the vegetables in the olive oil and spices, and then place a lid on the pan and let it all steam together for 5 minutes. Stir in the chopped tomatoes and turn up the heat to medium–high. Simmer for 20 minutes until the sauce is reduced and thick (similar to a pasta sauce) and not in any way watery. Season to taste with salt, pepper and sugar.

Finally, fold in the rinsed butterbeans and chopped dill and heat through gently. Serve with some crusty bread to mop up all the juices.

 Feel free to improvise here. Sometimes I make this casserole with carrots to give a sweeter mix; other times I use courgettes for a wetter pan; and then when I really want to pack the aniseed punch, I add a whole bulb of fennel. Take your pick.

Feasts for Friends

I can't help but plan parties. It's in my blood. I love a good feast. Plotting and inviting and shopping are my favourite things. It drives my husband Raf mad! When I was little we'd have big supper parties and everything was thought of. My father loved laying tables and lighting candles and polishing silver and my mum always cooked up a storm. It was always really exciting and everyone mucked in. I suppose I have inherited this love. But where my parents entertained in their way, we now have our own way too. Raf and I do the cooking together (sometimes with a little power struggle) and it tends towards Indian and Asian foods, as that's where we have travelled and those are the shops we live near. But the feelings of excitement are very much the same.

My dad's moulds and terrines were his signature and I have found myself recreating these dishes in my own way. I love pâtés because they look really impressive. They require planning and love and the finished article looks wonderfully medieval. The big feast is a great opportunity to try new recipes and twists. The chances are if you have invited a band of friends over you've got time on your hands to make some magic. Crème brulée? Try adding a little cardamom and mandarin and you will have a whole new exotic kind of custard pudding. My friend Alice always falls back on her mum Gillie's chilli con carne, but why not use whole hunks of brisket rather than mince, and add my brother Olly's American twist – some chocolate and coffee for added depth of flavour?

The important thing here is that everyone should be very well fed and the food should keep on flowing. At the beginning, the table should be heaving with your cooking and by the end, empty plates, dirty glasses and endless coffee cups should rule. Like Christmas, every day.

Only cook foods for your banquet that you actually want to prepare and eat. This isn't about impressing, it's about enjoying the process as much as the end result. If I cook things I don't want to eat, it never works out.

Formal dinners do not mean stuffy dinners. Allow the wine to flow and the dishes will follow. You don't have to be too structured – just bring your dishes to the table as each is ready.

If you are cooking a three course dinner, I would recommend that some of the recipes can be prepared in advance. So, if you are making the Tokyo Yakitori skewers, which need to be cooked just before serving, make sure that your pudding, perhaps trifle or chocolates, requires preparing well in advance. This way you won't be cooking everything at once and be chained to the cooker. You aren't feasting in order to pretend to be a chef. You are inviting your friends over so that you can actually talk to them.

Tokyo Yakitori

It wasn't until I actually made the long pilgrimage to Tokyo that I had some really good yakitori – chicken skewers. After a few hazy jet-lagged days bowling around this bizarre city we found a blue collar bar that served amazing bites of food and moreish sake. Datchi was the dishy chef with a quiff who taught us about real Japanese food: sea bream sashimi with the most delicate-smelling basil flowers; tenderest cow's heart and liver sashimi with a salty sesame oil pool for dipping; deep-fried chicken knuckles (like Japanese pork scratchings) and the most tender yakitori I have ever eaten. As he grilled and sliced morsels for us, he smoked and drank on the job, surrounded by his locals cheering and laughing. Now we make yakitori frequently. It is great as a simple starter for the beginnings of a feast, either under the grill in the kitchen or on the barbecue if you are gorging outside. For the Japanese 7 spice mix, head to your local Korean or Japanese supermarket. It is full of roasted orange or mandarin peel and black sesame seeds and is essential to bring this dish to completion.

Makes 12 skewers

100ml Japanese soy sauce
100ml mirin
2 tablespoons caster sugar
3 garlic cloves, peeled
500g chicken thigh fillets, skinned
Japanese 7 spice (or Togarashi spice)

You will need 12 long wooden skewers, soaked in water. Measure out the soy sauce, mirin and sugar in a small saucepan. Place the peeled garlic cloves on a chopping board and using the flat of a large knife, crush so that they are broken up. Add these to the pan and then bring to the boil. Turn the heat to low and simmer until the alcohol has cooked off and the sauce is a little thickened. Set this aside.

Preheat the grill to medium. Now for the chicken, trim off any fat and place each thigh out open on a board. Using the blunt edge of a knife give them a good bash to make the meat tender. Slice these into fine strips, less than 1cm in width. Now grab your soaked wooden skewers and sew the meat onto these to create a concertina. Don't pack the meat on too close or it will be harder to cook. Continue until you have used up all the meat and then place the skewers on a grill pan. Using a pastry brush, entirely coat the skewers in the prepared glaze and place under the grill. Remove from the grill every few minutes and add another layer of glaze, turning all the time until they are browned all over and a little sticky. This should take about 10 minutes. Serve with Japanese 7 spice dusted over the skewers and a small bowl of it on the side.

Classic Pork Terrine with Pernod

This classic – and very old-fashioned – recipe celebrates herbs and spices and is inspired by my dad and grandmother's shared love of coarse pâté. You can mix up and substitute the meats, and indeed the herbs and spices too, according to your fancy. I've added apricots for an extra-sweet surprise and texture. The pig's trotter is my addition to the family recipe – it drains and encases the pâté in a lovely brawn – but if you don't fancy it, the trotter is not essential. You can find trotters at a good Portuguese, Colombian or Brazilian butcher where they will slice them in half for you with a circular saw. And do your best to find allspice berries. They work fantastically well with the Pernod.

Serves 6–8

100ml Pernod
1 heaped teaspoon brown sugar
10 allspice berries, crushed in a pestle
   and mortar
10 black peppercorns, crushed in a pestle
   and mortar
freshly grated nutmeg
a handful of mixed fresh herbs, such as
   parsley, sage and thyme, finely chopped
sea salt
800g fatty minced belly pork
200g venison fillet, chopped into 1cm
   pieces
3 handfuls of fresh breadcrumbs
   (optional)
6 dried apricots, roughly chopped
250g unsmoked streaky bacon
5 bay leaves
1 pig's trotter, divided in half down the
   knuckle

Mix together the ingredients for the marinade in a jug – the Pernod, sugar, allspice berries, peppercorns, nutmeg, herbs and sea salt. Set aside. Using your hands, combine the minced pork, venison and breadcrumbs (if using) in a large bowl. Gradually knead in the marinade so that it is fully combined. Add the apricots and combine well.

Preheat the oven to 160°C/gas mark 3. Stretch each rasher of bacon over a knife handle to combat the retraction that will occur when the terrine is cooked. Arrange the bay leaves over the bottom of a 28cm springform loaf tin and then stripe the bacon over the top, leaving enough poking out at either side of the tin to fold over the top and enclose the terrine later. Carefully press the spiced meats into the tin and fold over the bacon to enclose the meat so that you end up with a wrapped parcel. Lay the bay leaves in a line over the bacon, top with the pig's trotter and then cover the whole thing with foil. Rest the tin in a baking tray. Half fill the tray with warm water so that it surrounds the pâté tin. Bake in the oven for 1½ hours, and remove the terrine to cool to room temperature. Place in the fridge overnight.

In the morning, unwrap your terrine. Remove the trotters from the top and release the sides of the tin. Flip out the terrine onto a chopping board or large plate to serve.

Chicken Liver Pâté with Brandy and Prunes

Chicken liver pâté is known for being a Christmas dish but frankly I can eat it every day of the year. This recipe is a family classic from my friend Rose, but I've adapted it by adding prunes, which give a lovely dark, sweet surprise. The one stipulation when you make pâté is to allow yourself plenty of time, as it does need to chill overnight, so bear this in mind if you're planning on making this for a dinner party or special occasion. It's easy peasy.

Serves 6 as a starter

250g unsalted butter
1 large onion, finely chopped
600g prepared chicken livers
Maldon sea salt
freshly ground black pepper
2 sprigs of fresh thyme
zest of ½ orange
100g stoned, ready-to-eat prunes
40ml cooking brandy or Marsala
1 teaspoon runny honey, to taste
 (optional)

Chop the butter into 3 equal pieces. Place one piece in a large wide frying pan on a low heat. When it has melted, add the onion and sweat for about 5 minutes or until it begins to soften and become translucent. Be careful not to brown them. Add the chicken livers, keeping the heat low so that they remain tender, and stir gently for 5 minutes until they turn pale grey on the outside. To check they are cooked, cut into one of the livers. It should be a perfect skin pink inside, but no darker. Turn the heat off and season with salt and lots of pepper. Strip the leaves off the thyme and add them to the pan with the orange zest. Set aside to cool for 10 minutes. Meanwhile, chop each prune into 4 pieces and set aside in a bowl.

Using a food-processor or a handheld blender, blitz the chicken liver mixture until it is really, really smooth. Add the reserved second chunk of butter and whizz this into the pâté before adding the brandy or Marsala. Taste and season more if necessary (sometimes it needs a teaspoon of runny honey). Fold the chopped prunes into the pâté and spoon into a shallow dish, about 25cm square or 6 large ramekins. Set aside to cool to room temperature.

Once the pâté has set, heat the remaining butter in a small pan on a low heat so that it is entirely melted but not browning. Take it off the heat. If you wish, you can clarify the butter by removing the paler milk solids with a slotted spoon, but I only do this if I have time. Spoon the melted butter over your pâté to create a seal. It looks really lovely if you drop a few thyme flowers over the butter lid. Transfer the pâtés to the fridge and leave to set overnight. Serve with some toasted slivers of bread and some cornichons if you wish.

Pink Peppercorn Pork Rillettes

Pork rillettes is a deliciously old-fashioned French dish, and each region has its own take on it. It can also be made from duck, goose or even fish. Pork rillettes is really just slow-cooked, potted and therefore preserved, not unlike potted shrimps. You can treat rillettes like a pâté, serving it as a starter or light summer lunch with cornichons, or you can use the system to preserve and keep aside some cooked meat to add to pastas or stews. Pink peppercorns are my twist. For me, they are essential here, giving a lovely, tingly aniseed aftertaste.

Serves 6–8

3 bay leaves
4 sprigs of thyme
1kg belly pork
3 teaspoons pink peppercorns
sea salt

Preheat the oven to 160°C/gas mark 3. Lay the bay leaves and thyme over the bottom of a baking dish big enough to house your pork. Place the belly pork inside and pour over 300ml water. Cover the dish with foil and bake for 3 hours.

Remove the belly pork from the oven and shred the meat finely with two forks, keeping aside the cooking liquor. Place the coarsely shredded meat in a mixing bowl and stir through the peppercorns and some salt. Tightly press the mixture into one shallow dish or divide between a selection of ramekins or bowls. Strain the cooking liquor through a sieve into a jug and discard the herbs. Pour the liquid over the packed meat and leave to cool. Place in the fridge to set overnight. Store in the fridge for up to a week.

Callaloo and Saint Paulin Soufflé

Callaloo is like Jamaican spinach, but it has its own distinct character. Milder and softer, with thick, delicate stalks, it is a staple West Indian green available at all good Jerk centres. This recipe hails direct from the lush Jamaican hillsides. We went to stay near Montego Bay with my fairy godmother Miss Tolerance. Every day her cooks offered up amazing half-Jamaican, half-European food. This callaloo soufflé was a major event. Wobbling and gigantic, it was gently placed in the middle of the table and we all dug into the soft, cloudy interior. It's hard to get good cheese in Jamaica, so I had smuggled out a kilo from the deli in my luggage to complete the dish.

Serves 8

180ml whole milk

2 bay leaves

a sprig of fresh thyme

30g butter

2 level tablespoons plain flour

125g Saint Paulin or Raclette, grated or cubed

200g cooked strained callaloo (or spinach), finely chopped

3 medium free-range eggs, separated

freshly ground black pepper

½ teaspoon ground nutmeg

> The main component of this dish is a light béchamel sauce, which you can make in advance if you want to prep ahead. Then all you need to do is fold in the stiff egg whites and bake for a matter of moments.

Preheat the oven to 200°C/gas mark 6. Half fill a large baking dish with water and place in the oven to warm up. Make sure it is large enough for whatever you are serving the soufflé in. Meanwhile, grease 8 8cm x 9cm x 6cm ramekins well, so that they are buttered right up to the lip. Set these aside.

To make the béchamel, heat the milk in a small pan with the bay leaves and thyme. Do not let it boil. Meanwhile, melt the butter in a medium pan on a low heat. When it has melted add the flour and whisk. It should be quite dry. Let this roux sweat in the pan to fully cook the flour. Remove the bay and thyme from the milk and gradually whisk this into the roux so that you have a thick, silky sauce. Keep the béchamel on the heat and add the cheese so that it melts. Now remove the pan from the heat and add the callaloo followed by the separated egg yolks. Beat to make sure that everything is well combined and then add some pepper and nutmeg. It shouldn't need salt as the callaloo and cheese are both salty.

Beat the egg whites vigorously so that they form stiff peaks. Mix a third of this into the béchamel to loosen it and then gently fold in the rest, being careful to maintain the air you have created. Spoon the mix into the ramekins so that each is three quarters full. Remove the warmed baking dish of water from the oven and place the ramekins in here, creating a bain-marie. Replace the soufflé-loaded dish in the oven for 15 minutes. The surface of the soufflés should be risen and crisp and golden but very responsive to the touch. Serve immediately before they lose their height.

Kedgeree

Kedgeree was traditionally a breakfast dish and a very colonial thing. I had it recently at my friend Flora Grimston's shooting party and was reminded of what a delicious and subtle dish it is. Being lightly spiced it conjures up the Raj and yet it is creamy and parsley-packed, which makes it very English. You could call it an original fusion dish. However, both my mother and I serve it for supper.

Serves 2–3

350g undyed smoked haddock, skin on
150ml whole milk
1 teaspoon whole fenugreek seeds
1 teaspoon whole black peppercorns
3 eggs
2 tablespoons vegetable oil
2 onions, finely chopped
15 whole cardamom pods
4 teaspoons whole coriander seeds
½ teaspoon mild curry powder
1 cinnamon stick
a pinch of saffron
2 bay leaves
lots of freshly ground black pepper
25g butter
200g basmati rice, rinsed under a
    running tap
2 tablespoons double cream
20g parsley, very finely chopped

To make the stock, skin the haddock, set aside the flesh and place the skin in a wide pan with 150ml water, the milk, fenugreek seeds and black peppercorns and set over a low heat. Poach gently for about 20 minutes and then remove from the heat. Meanwhile, cut the haddock into 2.5cm chunks. Strain 350ml of the stock through a nylon sieve and set aside for later.

To soft boil the eggs, place the eggs in a small saucepan and cover with cold water. Bring to the boil on a high heat, turn the heat down to medium and boil for 3½–4 minutes. Remove the eggs from the pan and place in a sink of cold water. When the eggs are cool, peel them and chop into quarters. Set aside.

To make the kedgeree, heat the vegetable oil in a big, wide, shallow pan. When it is piping hot, add the onions and turn the heat to medium. Fry the onions gently for 5 minutes or so until they start to soften. Measure out the cardamom and coriander seeds into a pestle and mortar and energetically grind. Remove the cardamom shells and add the ground spices and curry powder, cinnamon stick, saffron, bay leaves and black pepper to the pan. When the onions are nearly translucent, add a knob of butter to the pan and tip in the rice. Stir the rice to coat it in the butter and spices and then pour over 350ml of your reserved fish stock. Place on a high heat and simmer for about 5 minutes until all of the liquid has been absorbed. Mix in the cream and remove the pan from the heat. Scatter over the parsley, haddock and eggs and cover with a lid. Leave the kedgeree to steam quietly, off the heat, for 20 minutes by which time the fish should be perfectly cooked. Serve with plenty of freshly ground black pepper.

Twice-Cooked Belly Pork with Black Beans

Carnitas in Mexico is slow-roasted pork, and everywhere you go you can pick up tacos with this delicious sweet, wet meat inside. It can be poached first, before the slow roasting. This method is the starting point for this dish. The black bean stew is inspired by my friend Dani's recipe – her frequent family trips across the Mexican border made her passionate about the food and the importance of sourcing authentic ingredients. I've tried to adhere to in this in my recipe.

Serves 4–6

500g dried black beans, soaked in cold
   water overnight and rinsed thoroughly
1.5kg belly pork
2 star anise
1 teaspoon fennel seeds
8 juniper berries
8 allspice berries
1 teaspoon whole black peppercorns
2 bay leaves
4 dried red peppers
1 dried chipotle chilli
3 tablespoons vegetable oil
1 large onion, finely chopped
3 garlic cloves, peeled and crushed
3 small whole chillies
3 strips of lime zest, 1cm wide
sea salt
1 heaped teaspoon good-quality cocoa
   powder
zest and juice of 1 orange
2 tablespoons runny honey
½ teaspoon ground cloves
freshly ground black pepper
1 teaspoon sea salt

To garnish
3 spring onions, finely chopped
a handful of fresh coriander, torn
1 teaspoon finely chopped lemon verbena
   (or fresh oregano or majoram)

It is very important to soak the beans overnight. In the morning, rinse them thoroughly under a running tap to wash and set aside.

Place the belly pork in a medium saucepan and cover with water. Add the star anise, fennel seeds, juniper berries, allspice, peppercorns and bay leaves. Do not add salt. Bring to a very, very gentle simmer, place a lid on top and simmer gently for 20 minutes or until the meat is poached and tender. Remove the pork and place in a roasting tin, skin-side up, ready to transfer to the oven later. Strain the cooking liquor through a sieve into a clean pan.

To make the black bean stew, first rehydrate your peppers and chipotle: place them in a bowl, pour over enough boiling water to cover and set aside for 10 minutes, covered with clingfilm.

Meanwhile, heat the oil in a large saucepan. Add the onion and garlic and sweat on a medium–low heat for 5 minutes until translucent. Throw in the small whole chillies.

Return to the soaking peppers. Keeping the soaking water to one side, remove the peppers and chillies and pull off the stalks (these should come away easily). Deseed the pepper and cut into 1cm strips. Finely chop the chipotle, complete with seeds. Add to the pan and continue to sweat for a further 5 minutes, by which time the onions will have taken on a dark red tinge from the peppers and chilli. Add the soaked beans and pour over enough of the reserved cooking liquor to cover, so that the liquid comes about 2.5cm above the beans. Add the reserved pepper water and the strips of lime zest. Again, do not add salt.

Place a lid on the pan and simmer for 3 hours on a low heat, checking every half hour and stirring. You may need to add a little extra water if the beans start to stick or dry out. Only season the beans when they are entirely cooked and soft. You can blend a bowl of the beans and then return them to the pot to make it really creamy. I just use the back of a big spoon to mash them slightly. Lastly, blend in the cocoa powder and set the beans aside to reheat when the pork is ready.

Preheat the oven to 200°C/gas mark 6.

To make the marinade for the pork, grate the orange zest into a mixing jug, squeeze in the juice and add the honey, ground cloves and seasoning. Beat together with a fork so that you have a smooth marinade and rub over the pork. Add 100ml of the reserved cooking liquor (or some water) to the bottom of the roasting tin and cover the whole thing with foil. Place in the oven for an initial 30 minutes. Remove the foil and turn down the temperature to 150°C/gas mark 2. Return the pork to the oven for a further 1½ hours to caramelise the meat (2 hours in total).

To serve, spoon the warmed black beans into serving bowls, top with slices of crumbling belly pork and garnish with spring onions, coriander and lemon verbena.

I add lemon verbena to garnish at the end because it is the nearest I can get to Mexican oregano and adds a lovely citrus scent. Don't be shy of the fatty belly pork. It is the fat that gives such wonderful moisture to the meat.

Creole Chicken

This is the homecoming recipe of Jemima Mason. Whenever her sons Willy and Sam arrive back at Martha's Vineyard with their streams of friends, this is what she serves. Deep and American and a little spicy this is best served with cornbread and long grain rice. In the absence of Jemima's new world spices, we used paprika instead. It is the perfect substitute, being a little smoky.

Serves 6

1.5kg whole free-range chicken

3 tablespoons vegetable oil, plus a little extra for oiling your bird

table salt

1 teaspoon caster sugar

50g butter

2 onions, finely chopped

3 celery sticks, finely chopped

1 green pepper, deseeded and finely chopped

3 garlic cloves, peeled and crushed

3 bay leaves

½ teaspoon cayenne pepper

2 teaspoons dried oregano

½ teaspoon hot smoked Spanish paprika

6 tomatoes, finely chopped

2 x 400g cans chopped tomatoes

1 teaspoon caster sugar

freshly ground black pepper

1 teaspoon sea salt

 The key here is to really brown the first batch of onions. This gives the dish its lovely caramel depth.

Preheat the oven to 200°C/gas mark 6. Place your chicken in a roasting tray and pour some water in the base to stop it from sticking. Rub the bird all over with vegetable oil and then with 1 teaspoon salt and the sugar. Roast in the oven for 30 minutes, and then turn the heat down to 180°C/gas mark 4 and continue to roast for a further 40 minutes (1 hour and 10 minutes in total). Remove the chicken from the oven and set aside until cool enough to handle.

Meanwhile, heat the butter and 3 tablespoons vegetable oil in a large pan. Add half of the chopped onions and fry on a high heat until golden and starting to crisp. Remove from the pan with a slotted spoon and set aside on a plate. Turn the heat down low and add the rest of the onions, along with the celery, green pepper and garlic. Sweat the vegetables for 10 minutes until they are soft and translucent, and then stir in the reserved caramelised onions. Add the bay leaves, cayenne, oregano and paprika and stir well to coat the vegetables in the herbs and spices. When everything is well combined, add the fresh and canned tomatoes and season with sugar, pepper and salt. Be generous with the black pepper. Turn the heat to medium and simmer the sauce with the lid off for about 30 minutes until it has reduced by one-third and is sweet and thick.

Return to the chicken. When it is cool enough to handle, strip all the meat off the bird, being careful not to miss a scrap. Pile the meat into the sauce and give it a quick stir to combine. Serve with some cornbread on the side to mop up all the juices.

Fish Pie

This pie is a great take on a classic and hails from a Russian version. It started out life with Rosie Kitchen, who taught my mum to cook at Justin de Blanc's delicatessen, and the original recipe called for tapioca and fish in a pastry shell. My mum kept the format of a folded up pastry shell, but instead made a more classic béchamel sauce with fish and eggs. I have reverted to the original pie, but with brown rice instead of tapioca. This is testament to the constant evolution of food, tastes and wants.

Serves 6

50g brown rice
50g unsalted butter
1 teaspoon dill seeds
2 onions, finely chopped
250g oyster mushrooms, sliced into strips
2 garlic cloves, peeled and crushed
1 teaspoon sea salt
freshly ground black pepper
a small bunch of parsley, finely chopped
plain flour, for dusting
425g puff pastry
1 beaten egg (for the eggwash)
300g salmon, skinned and cut into 3cm
   chunks
300g monkfish, skinned and cut into 3cm
   chunks
3 soft-boiled eggs, peeled and halved

The look of this pie is banquet-impressive and the rice-laden filling is great if you are cooking on a shoestring: you won't need loads of expensive fish.

Preheat the oven to 220°C/gas mark 7 and grease a large, flat square baking tray. Place the brown rice in a medium pan and cover with lots of water. Bring to the boil and simmer for 30 minutes until the rice is tender. Drain and set aside. Melt the butter in a large pan over a moderate heat. Add the dill seeds and onions and sweat gently for 10 minutes until the onions become translucent. Add the oyster mushrooms – they will give out some water – and continue to fry gently until most of the moisture has evaporated. Add the garlic and seasoning and remove from the heat. Fold in the parsley and set aside. When the vegetables are cool, combine with the drained rice.

To assemble the pie, dust your worktop generously with flour. Place the pastry on the worktop and roll it out so that it is about 35cm square. Lift the pastry up, supporting it over your rolling pin, and transfer it to your greased baking tray. Generously brush the edges of the pastry with beaten egg. Heap half of the cooked rice in the centre of the pastry, scatter with the chunks of fish and boiled eggs and top with the rest of the rice. To close the pie, grab 2 opposite corners of the pastry and pinch together in the middle. Now grab the remaining 2 corners and pinch them together too to form a pouch. Use your finger and thumb to seal the pastry along each of the 4 seams and then brush all over with the eggwash. Bake in the oven for 30 minutes until the pie is golden, crisp and brittle on the surface. Remove from the oven and leave to rest for a few minutes before carving into wedges. Serve with a dressed watercress salad.

A Whole Chicken with Preserved Lemons and Black Cardamom Rice

This dish is somewhere between a casserole and a tagine. The flavours are smoky, citrine and far, far away. It is inspired by ingredients I found in a local shop specialising in Berber, Moorish and Arab foods, where I first stumbled across black cardamom seeds and really decent preserved lemons. The preserved lemons lend a jammy quality to the dish and the black cardamoms make a delicious smoke-infused rice.

Serves 6

For the chicken

4 tablespoons olive oil

1.5kg whole free-range chicken

2 medium onions, roughly chopped

3 carrots, peeled and roughly chopped

2 teaspoons ground cumin

1 teaspoon ground coriander

1 small chilli, finely chopped

1 x 400g can chopped tomatoes

2 tablespoons tomato purée

3 preserved lemons

2 tablespoons runny honey

1 x 800g can chickpeas, drained

sea salt

freshly ground black pepper

a handful of fresh flatleaf parsley, torn, to garnish

For the rice

750g basmati rice

6 black cardamom pods

3 star anise

1 teaspoon sea salt

Preheat the oven to 180°C/gas mark 4. Heat the oil in an ovenproof pan or casserole dish over a moderate heat. Place the chicken in the pan and brown it on all sides. Remove from the pan and set aside.

Add the onions and carrots to the pan and fry for a few minutes, stirring from time to time. Add the cumin, coriander and chilli and stir to thoroughly coat the vegetables. Fry on a low heat for 10 minutes, stirring, until the spices are strong smelling and the vegetables are slightly brown. Add the tomatoes, tomato purée, preserved lemons and honey. Give everything a good stir and then add 400ml water. Nestle the chicken among all the goodies and bring everything to the boil. Place a lid on the pan, put it in the oven and cook for 1 hour. Remove from the oven, add the chickpeas and stir well. Taste and season accordingly. Return to the oven for a further 45 minutes, uncovered, so that the sauce thickens slightly.

Meanwhile, place the rice in a large saucepan with 1.5 litres water, the black cardamoms, star anise and salt. Bring to the boil on a vigorous heat and cook for 10 minutes or until you can no longer see any bubbles or water in the rice. Turn the heat off, place a lid on top and set aside.

When the chicken is cooked, remove the dish from the oven and transfer the chicken to a carving board, being careful to drain off any liquid from inside the bird (I insert a fork under each drumstick and hang it upside down over the pan). Leave the chicken to rest, covered in foil, for 5 minutes before carving. To serve, fluff up the rice with a fork and scatter the torn parsley over the carved chicken and chickpeas.

Boned Stuffed Chicken for a Summer Supper

My mum made this dish for parties when I was little and finally this year she taught me how to do the boning, which is no mean feat. Once you know how to do this, you can stuff a chicken with whatever you want. Sausagemeat is one of the best fillings because it is firm and keeps the bird's shape. The great thing about roasting a chicken this way is that without all the bones you can carve it like a piece of ham and unveil the beautiful marbled colours within. I've added kale and chorizo to my version. The kale gives a gorgeous woody garden flavour and the chorizo beautifully infuses the stuffing with paprika and a hint of Spain.

Serves 6

1.5kg free-range chicken, boned by the
 butcher
100g kale
2 tablespoons olive oil, plus extra for
 rubbing into the chicken
1 red pepper, deseeded and finely sliced
1 yellow pepper, deseeded and finely
 sliced
1 small mild parrilla cooking chorizo
350g good sausagemeat
30g curly parsley, roughly chopped
1 egg, beaten
Maldon sea salt
freshly ground black pepper

You can serve this dish with bowls of soup and loads of different big dishes – I serve the boned chicken cold, but you can serve it warm if you prefer.

Lay your chicken out on a large chopping board with the cavity side up ready to fill. Wash the kale and place it, wet, in a medium saucepan on a low heat. Place the lid on top and wilt for 5 minutes or so until it has reduced. Set aside to cool and then roughly chop. Heat the olive oil in a wide frying pan on a low heat. Add the peppers, turning them frequently in the oil until they are soft – about 20 minutes. To make them super silky, you may wish to add a little water to the pan and let it simmer away until it has evaporated. Set aside with the kale.

Preheat the oven 180°C/gas mark 4. Split the chorizo and finely chop the meat. Place in a large mixing bowl with the sausagemeat, parsley and beaten egg. Season, roll up your sleeves and give everything a really good kneading. Once the kale and peppers are cool (you don't want them to start cooking the meat), add them to the mixture and give it one last churn.

Carefully fill the boned chicken with your stuffing, being careful to keep the shape of the bird. Pull together the opening and sew up the cavity. Place the stuffed bird in a roasting tray, seam-side down, and add some water in the base of the tray to stop it sticking. Rub some olive oil and salt into the skin and roast in the oven for 1½ hours.

If you want to eat the chicken straight away, leave it to rest, covered in foil, for at least 10 minutes before carving. If you are going to have it cold, leave overnight in the fridge to feast on the next day.

Lamb Fillet Pilau with Caramelised Onions and Barberries

This recipe, silken and warming, like many of my favourite dishes, comes from *The Moro Cookbook*. However, as is characteristic for me, I have merged a few ideas here. It is partly Sam and Sam Clark's saffron rice recipe but I've added lamb fillet too. The two most important things when making this recipe are to make amazing sweet caramelised onions and to find a good Middle Eastern shop that sells barberries. These are tiny, tart and sweet and totally seal the deal.

Serves 4

For the onions
1 large onion, finely sliced
200ml vegetable oil

For the lamb pilau
500g lamb fillet, diced
3 tablespoons olive oil
1 teaspoon ground cinnamon
1 teaspoon whole cumin seeds
1 teaspoon whole fennel seeds
1 large onion, finely diced
200g basmati rice, soaked for a few hours
a small pinch of saffron
2 tablespoons dried barberries or
    cranberries
200ml vegetable stock
40g sliced almonds, toasted

To make the caramelised onions be sure that the onion is uniformly finely sliced so that it fries evenly. This is best achieved in a Magimix or using a mandolin slicer. Heat the oil in a wok or deep frying pan on a high heat until it is smoking. Now reduce the heat to a moderate flame and add the onion in batches. Stir and toss, being careful not to be in the direction of any spitting oil. When the onions are golden and getting firm remove from the pan with a slotted spoon and set aside on some kitchen paper.

To make the lamb, marinate by tossing it in 2 tablespoons of the olive oil and the ground cinnamon, cumin and fennel seeds. Set this aside for a couple of hours.

Heat a large pan on a moderate flame and add the lamb. After a few minutes add the diced onion and turn the heat to low. Place a lid on the pan and let the lamb gently warm through for 15 minutes so that it is only just cooked – it should be just sealed and pale and tender.

Finally, for the rice, heat the remaining tablespoon of oil in a large pan on a medium flame. Add the rice, saffron and barberries and let these all fry, stirring until the rice is becoming a little golden. Reduce the heat and add the lamb and its juices, fully combining. Add enough stock to cover the cover the lamb and come about 1cm above the top of the pilau. Place a lid on the pan and bring it to a simmer for 8 minutes. Then remove the lid and let it sit for a further 5 minutes. This will allow excess steam to escape and stop it becoming sticky. To serve, scatter over the onions and some toasted almonds.

Brisket Chilli con Carne with Coffee

I first started making this tex-mex crowd-pleaser because of my friend Alice. Chilli con carne is her mother's fallback classic, ideal for feeding a load of guests. I can't think of many who don't like a bowl of chilli and a baked potato at a packed party. I've changed the blueprint recipe by using whole chunks of brisket rather than minced beef. When this cooks down it falls apart and is deliciously succulent. I've also added coffee and chocolate on my brother's advice, to give a rich depth to the finished dish.

Serves 8

2.2kg beef brisket
200ml strong coffee
3 large dried chillies
4 tablespoons vegetable oil
2 teaspoons ground cumin
1 teaspoon mild Hungarian paprika
1 teaspoon hot smoked Spanish paprika
1 teaspoon dried oregano
2 bay leaves
2 cinnamon sticks
2 red onions, finely chopped
10 garlic cloves, peeled and crushed
4 x 400g cans chopped tomatoes
2 tablespoons runny honey
3 red peppers, deseeded and sliced
1 x 400g can black beans, drained
1 x 400g can kidney beans, drained
2 tablespoons plain chocolate callets

To garnish
5 spring onions, finely chopped
200g mild Cheddar, grated
40g fresh coriander, roughly chopped
4 limes, cut into wedges

Prepare the brisket by cutting it into 2cm dice. Set aside. Make a strong brew of coffee. Place the dried chillies in a bowl, pour over the hot coffee and leave to rehydrate whilst you get on with everything else.

Heat the oil in a very large pan over a moderate heat. Add the cumin, paprikas, oregano, bay leaves and cinnamon sticks. Let them fry briefly to release their deep aromas into your kitchen, and then turn the heat down low and add the onions and garlic. Sweat for 5 minutes until they start to soften, stirring frequently. When the onions are translucent, add the canned tomatoes and honey. Bring to the boil and simmer gently for 30 minutes. Stir in the chopped brisket, fit a lid on the pan and simmer gently for 2 hours. Add the peppers and beans, the steeped chillies and coffee, and continue to simmer for a further hour. Just before serving, mix in the chocolate so it has just long enough to melt.

Serve with rice or baked potatoes and separate little bowls of goodies to sprinkle on the top.

 Serve with lots of garnish – for an informal dinner party you can put the garnishes in little dishes and let your guests help themselves to what they fancy.

Pheasant with Porcini Mushrooms

We used to eat pheasant a lot when I was little. Mum would roast it, and to be honest, I always hated it. I was in constant fear of chewing on the gunshot. But then Stefano Paolini, a loyal customer at Rosie's shared his mum's recipe with me, fresh from Emilia-Romagna. When Stefano was a boy, September to November meant mushroom-picking season. They would drive to a forest and, armed with a basket, a knife and a strong stick, begin their hunt. After combing the forest for hours they would return home with a healthy gathering of porcini, boletus and chanterelles.

Serves 2

300g fresh porcini mushrooms (*Boletus edulis*), or 20g dried porcini if you can't find fresh

1 pheasant, cut into leg, thigh and breast pieces

plain flour, for dusting

6 tablespoons olive oil

150ml red table wine

50g butter

1 medium onion, finely chopped

1 bay leaf

100g pancetta, cut into lardons

2 ripe tomatoes

200ml vegetable stock

300g valsugana polenta

30g parsley, washed

1 garlic clove, peeled

Maldon sea salt

freshly ground black pepper

If you are using dried mushrooms, soak them in a small bowl of boiling water for about 25 minutes until the pieces become plump. Drain by squeezing out the water with your hands. If you are using fresh mushrooms, wipe away any excess dirt with a damp cloth (do not wash them in water) and set aside.

Dust the pheasant pieces in plain flour. Heat 2 tablespoons of the olive oil in a non-stick frying pan over a moderate heat. Gently fry the pheasant on both sides until golden brown – this should take about 10 minutes. Remove the pheasant and set aside on a plate. Add the red wine to the pan to deglaze and reduce the liquid by half.

Heat 3 tablespoons of the olive oil and the butter in a large, cast-iron pot over a moderate heat. When it has melted, add the onion and fry for 5 minutes until soft. Add the bay leaf and pancetta and fry for 5 minutes until light golden brown. Dice the mushrooms into small pieces. Add them to the pot and sauté for 10 minutes until most of the water has evaporated. To prepare the tomatoes, score the stem end with a cross and place in a small bowl. Cover with boiling water, leave to stand for 10 minutes and then peel away the skins. Slice the peeled tomatoes in half and scoop out the seeds, and then finely chop the flesh and add to the pot. Nestle the pheasant portions in the pan and pour over enough stock to cover and the red wine reduction. Place a lid on the pot, bring to the boil and then turn down the heat to its lowest setting. Simmer gently for 1 hour 30 minutes, stirring every 20 minutes and topping up the stock from time to time to keep the pheasant moist. Remove

from the heat when the meat starts to come away from the bone and all of the stock is used up.

Meanwhile, prepare the polenta according to the instructions on the packet. For the finale, place the parsley, garlic and the remaining tablespoon olive oil in a blender and blitz until you have a firm salsa. Five minutes before you serve the pheasant, add a teaspoon of the salsa to the pot and stir to combine. Season to taste with salt and pepper, but go easy on the salt because the pancetta and stock will be quite salty already.

Perfect Poached Pears

Being poached in red wine, this pudding is naturally quite Christmassy. The spiced infusion seems to herald woolly socks, pumped up heating and cosy evenings in. I've loosened the red wine a little by adding water, which stops it from becoming too rich. Serve with vanilla yogurt.

Serves 4

4 firm pears, peeled
450ml red wine
250ml water
300g caster sugar
8 whole green cardamom pods
½ teaspoon ground cinnamon
1 bay leaf
a strip of lemon zest
a disc of ginger, 4mm thick
½ vanilla pod

Place the pears on their sides in a medium saucepan with a matching lid. Pour over the wine and water and then half the sugar and the remaining ingredients. Fit the lid and place the pan on a medium heat so that it reaches a simmer. Reduce the heat to low and simmer for 25 minutes, turning three times during the course of cooking so that the pears become stained all over. Allow them to cool in their juices for an hour or so with the lid on.

To serve, drain the pears and plate them up. Strain the poaching juices into a pan and add the remaining caster sugar. Heat this vigorously for a few minutes until it is bubbling and becoming syrupy. Spoon this over the pears and offer up with vanilla yogurt.

Cardamom Tea Rice Pudding

There are endless ways to jazz up rice pudding and make this comforting, familiar dish new again. When I was little, Mum often made rice pudding, letting it bake for hours in her Rayburn range. It feels like a really nourishing thing to bake, which is ideal when the nights are long and your body is yearning for nourishment. This scented alternative using cardamoms smells far, far away from the school rice pudding we can all remember.

Serves 6

6 green cardamom pods
1 cardamom tea bag
1 English breakfast tea bag
370ml whole milk
1 x 410g can evaporated milk
20g butter
110g pudding rice
35g caster sugar
1 heaped teaspoon ground nutmeg

Preheat the oven to 170°C/gas mark 3½.

Steep the cardamom pods and tea bags in a little boiling water for at least an hour. Remove the tea bags, leaving the cardamom pods. In an ovenproof dish measuring 25 x 35cm, mix together the tea infusion with the whole milk, evaporated milk, butter, pudding rice, sugar and nutmeg. Bake for at least an hour, stirring every 20 minutes.

Serve with some stewed fruit or a spoonful of warm rhubarb jam.

Most important here is to use freshest green cardamom pods (not dusty old nuggets from the back of your spice cupboard) and steep the tea for a long while.

Trifle Two ways: Summer Trifle

Everyone loves a trifle. It is the British tiramisu and conjures up images of long summer lunches and excessively enjoyable gluttony. I have added pomegranate to my classic summer trifle, which gives a lovely juicy unorthodox crunch. Andrew Murray-Watson sent me his mum's traditional trifle recipe, which is heavy on the almonds but doesn't contain fruit and is drunk with sherry. In the winter version I have adopted his keen use of almond and sherry. Using tinned fruit makes a good alternative for winter festivities. Make sure you have a nice deep bowl, preferably glass so you can see the delicious layers of excess.

Serves 8

250g Madeira cake
4 almond fingers
250ml cream sherry
450ml double cream
300ml whole milk
6 egg yolks
2 tablespoons cornflour
30g caster sugar
½ teaspoon vanilla extract
1 ripe pomegranate
500g fresh summer berries
40g toasted flaked almonds

Break up the Madeira cake and almond fingers into a mixing bowl and cover them in the sherry. Let this sit and the flavours merge. Meanwhile, heat 300ml of the double cream and the milk over a moderate heat. Remove from the heat just before it comes to the boil. In a bowl, whisk together the egg yolks, cornflour, sugar and vanilla until they form a pale paste. Still using your whisk, slowly combine the hot milk with the egg mixture and beat until smooth. Return the custard to the pan, set over a very low heat and stir continuously with a wooden spoon until the sauce thickens. When the custard is thick enough to coat the back of your spoon – you want it to be fairly thick – take it off the heat and set aside to cool slightly and start to set.

You will need a nice deep glass bowl to assemble the trifle in. Place half of the soaked cake in the bottom of the bowl.

Remove the pomegranate seeds from the whole fruit and scatter half of them over the top. Layer on half of the summer berries and finish with half of the custard. Set aside in the fridge to firm up slightly for an hour. You can then add the remaining cake mix, followed by the fruit and custard layers. To finish, whip the remaining cream until it forms soft peaks. Spoon over the trifle and scatter with the almonds. Set in the fridge for a few hours to firm up completely.

Trifle Two ways: Winter Trifle

Serves 6

250g dark fruit cake

200ml cream sherry

450ml double cream

300ml whole milk

4 egg yolks

2–3 teaspoons cornflour

30g caster sugar

½ teaspoon vanilla extract

2 x 300g cans gooseberries, drained

zest of 1 orange

40g toasted flaked almonds

Make in the same way as the previous recipe, substituting fruit cake for the Madeira cake and almond fingers. Layer up the gooseberries and orange segments with the cake and custard and top with whipped cream and the flaked almonds.

Muscovado Amaretti Yogurts

This recipe is beautifully simple and consists of beaten cream with yogurt folded in. What I love about this pudding is that it is fresh and light at the same time as being brilliantly decadent. I suppose it is a bit like a deconstructed syllabub. These will take you a matter of moments to create and they are delicious the next day for breakfast too – when you are clearing up from the party the night before!

Serves 6

300ml double cream

350g Greek yogurt

zest of 1 orange

75g amaretti biscuits, roughly crushed

3 tablespoons dark muscovado sugar, for
 sprinkling

Whip the double cream in a large mixing bowl until it is light and thick. Fold in the yogurt, grate in the orange zest and finally carefully fold in the crushed amaretti biscuits. Spoon the mixture into a medium-sized dessert bowl or 6 glasses and crumble over a little muscovado sugar. If possible, leave to stand for a few hours before serving to allow the muscovado to melt and the orange to infuse the cream.

Hazelnut Meringue

This recipe comes from my in-laws and everyone waxes lyrical about this nutty summer pudding. My husband's grandmother, Joan Hendry, started cooking it in the 1960s after attending a Fanny Craddock demonstration. The hazelnuts in this version lend an almost chocolatey quality. Try mixing it up with different components – a raspberry coulis? Some grated chocolate? A little booze in the whipped cream?

Serves 6

4 egg whites

2 tablespoons vegetable oil, for greasing

125g hazelnuts

250g caster sugar

a few drops of vanilla extract

1 teaspoon white wine vinegar

275ml double cream

1 punnet of raspberries (about 200g)

icing sugar, for dusting

Bring the egg whites to room temperature. Line the base of 2 cake tins with foil. Grease the sides and the foil with vegetable oil. Toast the nuts until they are golden. My father-in-law does this in a low oven (120°C/gas mark ½), but I don't trust myself to do it that way and prefer to toast them in a dry pan over a low heat on the hob. Tip them onto a plate to cool, and then pulse them in a food-processor until they are ground but still have some slightly chunky bits. Then turn the oven up to 200°C/gas mark 6.

Place the egg whites in a large bowl and whisk until they are super stiff. Gradually fold in the caster sugar, then the vanilla and vinegar and finally the nuts – do this carefully as you don't want to lose any air. Divide the mixture into 2 20cm round cake tins and bake in the oven for 10 minutes. Keeping the door closed, turn the temperature down to 170°C/gas mark 3 and cook for a further 25–30 minutes. Do not open the oven for the entirety of the baking. Remove the meringues from the oven and leave to cool in their tins. Only attempt to remove them from their tins when they are stone cold.

Whip the double cream in a bowl until it forms soft peaks. Add the raspberries and continue beating until they are all whizzed up in the cream and the stained cream forms firm peaks. Spread the mixture over the first meringue and seal with the second meringue on top. Dust with icing to serve.

Black Rice Pudding

This is a brilliant take on our classic nursery pudding, which I stumbled upon by quizzing the girls in my local Chinese supermarket (a great way of getting new ideas). It hails from Asia and is more nutty than our slightly pappy relative version. However, what it shares with British rice pudding is the inclusion of nutmeg, which lends a delicate spicing that I just can't get enough of — whichever way you want to eat your rice pudding.

Serves 6 hungry people

450g black rice (available from Asian supermarkets)

1 litre coconut milk

zest of 1 lime

½ teaspoon freshly grated nutmeg

110g unrefined sugar – either jaggery or palm sugar (available from Asian supermarkets)

crème fraîche and fresh mango slices, to serve

Place the rice in a sieve and rinse under cold running water. Tip into a large saucepan, add the coconut milk, lime zest and nutmeg and bring slowly to the boil. Turn the heat down as low as you can and place a lid on top. Simmer for about an hour, until most of the milk has been absorbed. Grate in the unrefined sugar and continue to heat for just long enough for this to dissolve. Taste to check the balance of sugar and lime, just as you would when you are seasoning a savoury dish. It should have a slightly nutty texture and be gently sweet. Serve with crème fraîche and sliced mango.

 I have suggested serving this dish with crème fraîche, which is totally unorthodox – being French – but I really like the tart edge that it offers in contrast to the rich coconut milk. You are aiming for the pudding rice to be nutty with a bite – similar to risotto – not the creamy texture you would expect from traditional rice pudding.

Amazing Truffles

Quite simply a chocolate ganache covered in cocoa, the truffle is a very French delicacy. My friend Steph and I have done a load of supper clubs together and each time she has made these amazing truffles to go with coffee. I tease her that she has hippy tastes and sprouts seeds but actually she is a genius. We have played around with the flavourings so you have a choice of varieties to choose from here. The rosewater gives a lovely Eastern infusion, like a very upmarket Turkish delight. But the salted honey truffles are definitely my favourite.

Makes 25

200g dark chocolate (at least 70 per cent cocoa solids)
200ml double cream
½ –1 teaspoon rosewater
2 heaped tablespoons good-quality cocoa powder, to dust
edible glitter, to decorate

If you don't fancy making pudding, truffles are ideal in that they give the pretence of effort without much elbow grease. Alternatively, they work really well as a sweet present.

To make rosewater truffles, start by finely chopping the chocolate into a large mixing bowl. Heat the cream in a medium saucepan over a moderate heat until it is nearly at boiling point. Pour the hot cream over the shards of chocolate and stir carefully until all the chocolate has melted into the cream. Do not beat as this will alter the texture of the truffles. Add the rosewater and mix thoroughly. Taste in case you want to add more flavourings. Set aside to cool slightly, and then refrigerate until firm.

To fashion the truffles, dust a large plate with cocoa powder and glitter and get another plate ready to store the truffles on. Using a teaspoon, gouge out a small amount of the chocolate cream and roll in the palm of your hand to make a ball. Roll in the cocoa and glitter until it is completely coated and glistening, and then place on the clean plate. Repeat until all of the chocolate cream has been used up. Store in the refrigerator for up to a week.

Variations
Salted Honey Truffles: Add 1 teaspoon of really good sea salt and 2 teaspoons strong-tasting flower honey instead of the rosewater.

Zesty Orange Truffles: Add the zest of 1 orange instead of the rosewater.

Campari and Orange Jellies

Whenever my grandmother had big lunch parties she would make us kids jelly full of suspended fruit. I wanted to grow this dish up by adding some tasty liquor. On my last French trip I drank a lot of Campari with blood orange. It's a perfect accompaniment to a game of table tennis and evening sun. Not sweet, a little sour, and full of aromatic punch, Campari and orange is a very intricate drink. I've used those same cocktail ingredients to spice up my granny's classic.

Serves 6

5 gelatine leaves
1 x 290g can grapefruit segments
400ml blood orange juice (or normal
   orange juice)
2 tablespoons caster sugar
150ml Campari

Chop the gelatine leaves into 2.5cm square pieces, place in a bowl and cover with a little warm water to begin the dissolving process. Drain the tinned fruit and arrange in the bottom of 6 pretty glasses.

Heat the blood orange juice with the sugar until the sugar has dissolved. Bring to the boil, and then take the pan off the heat. Leave for a few minutes to cool down slightly. Add the gelatine and stir well to ensure it has dissolved completely. Pour in the Campari and taste to check it is sweet enough – it should be sour with a hint of sweetness. Pour the mixture over the grapefruit pieces and set aside to cool. Refrigerate until really firm and serve with cups of fresh mint tea.

Homemade Honeycomb

I love this classic treat, sold in bags at the fairground. It is a great way of making a pudding without too much fuss. Almost like you are serving up a little broken piece of childhood heavy with memories of tattoos and tinkling merry-go-round tunes.

Makes a big baking tray

vegetable oil, for greasing
6 tablespoons golden syrup
300g caster sugar
4 teaspoons baking powder

Line a baking tray with baking paper and lightly oil. Measure out the golden syrup and sugar into a large wide saucepan. Place this on a moderate heat. It will gradually all incorporate and melt together. When it has been bubbling gently for a few minutes it should start to turn golden. At the point where it is a red brown at the edges, swirl the pan a few times and then take it off the heat. Now quickly add the baking powder. Use a whisk to swiftly beat together. It will bubble in a very satisfying way. Pour out immediately onto your lined tray and let it set for a few hours in a cool, dry place. When it is firm and brittle, turn it out and place in a bag. Bash it up with a rolling pin and then tip the shards of joy out into a bowl to serve with coffees.

You can also keep the honeycomb to add to cake icings or crumble or ice cream. However, it does not fare well if damp so store it in an airtight container.

Weekend Cooking

Cooking on a Sunday is a very different affair to cooking during week. For me it follows two distinct paths: preserving and baking. The first, preserving, is about long and committed cooking, not immediately gratifying but ultimately hugely rewarding. It requires patience and love, something that took me a long time to work out.

Preserving for the winter – making chutneys and jams and jarring in general – is a well-worn tradition. Throughout history, people have preserved summer and autumn produce in preparation for the coming cold months. In doing so, the dark days are not quite so dark. There are sweet and condensed chutneys that utilise all sorts of spoils –marrows, tomatoes, cauliflowers or onions, which can be perked up with spices, nuts, dried fruit and chillies. And there are classics like apple jelly, which can either be kept simple or jazzed up with chillies and spices to add deeper, more complex layers. And, of course, there are cordials, wines and jams too.

My dad was a big fan of the home brew. Every time we opened the larder we would be greeted by rows of massive bottles quietly bubbling away. They rarely came to anything, but we always found them very exciting. Slightly more successful was his sloe gin, perfect to sip on Christmas morning while opening presents or, as I do now, to whizz up with frozen plums for a delicious granita. Mum was a great preserver too. She always seemed to be piling something into a muslin bag ready to hang over the kitchen table. Today, I find myself doing much the same thing. My kitchen is smaller, and I haven't acquired all the best equipment yet, but it's a lifetime's work.

The other aspect of the Sunday cook-off, and slightly more instantaneous in pleasure, is baking. I love cakes, and bake them often. Cakes are the perfect excuse to lure friends round for tea on a Sunday. The patience here is in letting them bake. Many a cake is ruined by quick, too hot baking or just not long enough in the oven. The trick is to make your cake and leave it alone. Baking is such an enjoyable way of giving too. My friend Sophie Moody, a mother of two and a fine and famous baker, takes great pleasure from making her lemon drizzle for friends as a present. You just can't buy that.

When you are making preserves, get your sterilising on lock-down. Whenever I cut corners with this, it backfires.

Once you have mastered the art of preserving, your storecupboard will take on a whole new life. Every meal will be vitalised by your accompaniments – just buy some English ham and serve it with a chutney or jelly.

Learn to love kneading when baking bread. It may seem laborious, it will create elasticity in your loaf and make a far superior dough.

Baking a Sunday afternoon cake provides enjoyment for the next few days – I leave a cake on the table and slice off a sliver each time I make a mug of tea – greedy but great.

Only ice a cake when it is entirely cold. Otherwise the warmth from the cake will melt your frosting.

Always line your baking tin when baking cakes. It will make the releasing so much easier.

Lemongrass Cordial

When my parents were first married, they lived in a cottage in Norfolk. It had no running water (not even a loo) and was freezing cold and pretty derelict. This was when they started foraging – nettle soup, wild mushrooms and, in the summer, elderflower cordial (due to the abundance of elder trees in Norfolk). I've adapted it here by using lemongrass, which I can get all year round from my local Asian store. It is lemony, but also a little bit tingly and hot. Now there is never any shortage of cordial in my home.

Makes about 500ml

zest of 1 lemon
250ml lemon juice (about 6 lemons)
4 sticks of lemongrass
1 teaspoon citric acid
230g caster sugar

You will need 1m untreated muslin and a 500ml bottle with a lid.

To make the cordial, put the lemon zest into a measuring jug and juice the lemons into the jug to give you 250ml lemon juice. Place the lemongrass on a chopping board and bash thoroughly with a wooden spoon. This will break it open so that its flavour really infuses the cordial. Place the lemongrass in a medium saucepan, pour in the lemon juice, add the citric acid and caster sugar and top up with 250ml water. Place the pan over a moderate heat and bring to the boil, stirring to dissolve the sugar. Remove from the heat and set aside to infuse for 6 hours.

Drape the muslin over a sieve. Set the sieve over a large measuring jug or bowl and carefully pour in the cordial to give you a clear syrup. Throw away 3 of the lemongrass sticks and keep 1 to one side.

To sterilise your glass bottle, immerse the bottle and the lid in a large pan of water and bring to a rumbling boil. Remove carefully and drain.

Insert the reserved lemongrass stick into the sterilised bottle and top up with the cordial. If possible, leave the cordial to infuse in the fridge for a few days before drinking. Serve 1 part cordial to 4 parts water. For a really summery vibe, add some edible flowers, slices of lime and a fresh lemongrass stick to the pitcher.

Kaffir Lime Cordial

This follows a very similar method to the lemongrass cordial. Kaffir lime leaves are available in large bags from any good Asian supermarket. You won't need a whole bag for this recipe, but the good news is they freeze brilliantly. The Aromatic Chicken Noodle Soup on page 16 also calls for kaffir lime leaves so you might have an abundance of lime leaves at some point. Why not make that one evening, and then you can spend your weekend using up the rest of the leaves with this recipe?

Makes about 750ml

zest of 1 lime
250ml citrus juice (about 10 limes and
   1 lemon)
15g kaffir lime leaves
230g caster sugar
1 teaspoon citric acid

You will need 1m untreated muslin and a 750ml bottle with a lid.

Grate the zest of one of the limes into a medium saucepan. Pour in the citrus juice and add the lime leaves. Add the caster sugar, 250ml water and the citric acid. Bring to the boil, and then simmer for about 10 minutes until the sugar has dissolved and the lime leaves have infused the juice. Set aside to steep for 6 hours.

Drape your muslin over a sieve and set over a large measuring jug or bowl. Pour in the cordial to give you a nearly clear syrup. Set aside a couple of the lime leaves to place in your cordial bottle.

To sterilise your glass bottle, immerse the bottle and lid in a large pan of water and bring to a rumbling boil. Remove carefully and drain. Insert the reserved lime leaves into the neck of the bottle and top up with the cordial. Store in the refrigerator for a few days before drinking to allow the flavours to infuse. Serve 1 part cordial to 4 parts water. For a really summery vibe, add some edible flowers, slices of lime and fresh lime leaves to your pitcher.

Chilli Sherry

Hailing from Trinidad, this West Indian recipe has been handed down the generations of the Carey family, who use it as a secret ingredient on everything from risotto and bolognese to shepherd's pie. Their version uses a ratio of 75:25 of dry to medium sherry, however I've used a nice Manzanilla that should work out the same. You can store it in a decanter to keep near the kitchen table and it also makes a great present at Christmas.

Makes about 750ml

750ml medium dry sherry, such as
  Manzanilla
3 red bird's eye chillies, halved
3 green bird's eye chillies, roughly
  chopped into 1cm pieces

Pour out all of the sherry from the bottle into a jug. Carefully sterilise the bottle by filling it to the brim with boiling water. Also cover the lid with boiling water too. Let it sit for a moment, and then empty out the water.

Stuff the chillies down the neck of the bottle and top up with your sherry. There will probably be some left over, which you can drink as you work. Carefully replace the lid on the bottle and leave for a few days for the chillies to infuse the sherry. Store for up to 4 months.

Keep the bottle on the kitchen table and add to just about everything! You may want to invest in an olive oil pourer for the top of the bottle so you can pour it out easily.

Try this sherry in salad dressings too. I recently made a classic mozzarella, basil and tomato salad and, in the absence of any vinegar, used this sherry instead. It made a subtle and lovely change.

Chilli Oil

The sign of a grown-up, in my book, is a person who not only cooks every day, but someone who also makes preserves for the storecupboard. This chilli oil is straightforward stuff to make, and actually it's pretty hot. It will keep for a few months, if it lasts you that long! Although common in Asia, I've gone for a more European version here using olive oil.

Makes about 500ml

25 fresh red chillies, each about a finger's length
1 x 500ml bottle of olive oil, preferably with a plastic pourer in the neck

Preheat your oven to 100°C/gas mark ¼. Find a baking tray with a fitted rack (most good new ovens come with these) and scatter the chillies over the top. Spread out evenly so that none of them are touching. Place the tray in the oven for 4 hours, but keep a close eye on it – you don't want the chillies to burn or roast, just to dehydrate. Leave to cool. You will only need half of the dried chillies (about 25g) for this recipe. Store the rest in a sealed bag ready for adding to curries and pasta sauces.

Remove the plastic pourer from the neck of your bottle and pour out all but 2 tablespoons of the olive oil into a measuring jug. Take about 25g of the dried chillies and cut off and discard the stalks. Finely slice the flesh and feed into the oil bottle. Top up the bottle with the olive oil, replace the plastic pourer and lid and turn the bottle upside down to totally emerge the pieces of chilli. Set aside to infuse for about a week before using. Store out of direct sunlight for up to 6 months.

Ketchup
2011

Ketchup
2011

Ketchup

Ketchup
2011

Ketchup
2011

Classic Tomato Ketchup

Whilst the yield for this recipe isn't really high, the results are just fantastic. Who could top homemade ketchup? This is a different beast to the shop-bought stuff and has a much fresher taste and tang. I have given a basic recipe here, but you can add all sorts: fresh dill, fresh basil, extra chillies, red peppers. Have a play.

Makes 3 x 500ml bottles

3 whole star anise
2 teaspoons whole cloves
1 cinnamon stick
1 teaspoon dill seeds
1 teaspoon cumin seeds
850ml malt vinegar
2 dried chillies, finely chopped
700g onions, peeled and finely chopped
3kg ripe tomatoes, quartered
1 teaspoon sea salt
700g golden caster sugar

Place the star anise, cloves, cinnamon, dill seeds and cumin seeds in 50cm untreated muslin and tie it tightly so nothing can escape. Place in a large pan with one-third of the vinegar and the chillies, onions, tomatoes and salt. Simmer gently for 50 minutes until everything is really soft, stirring frequently. Add the remainder of the vinegar and also the sugar. Continue to simmer and stir for a further hour, or until the ketchup is thick and jammy. Remove the muslin full of spices. Blitz the contents of the pan using a handheld blender, and then pass the ketchup through a sieve into a bowl. It should be silky smooth in texture.

I like to store my ketchup in nice beer bottles, but you can use whatever glass containers you have. To sterilise your bottles, immerse them in a large pan of water and bring to a rumbling boil. Remove carefully and drain. Pour in the hot ketchup using a funnel and seal immediately. Store in the fridge.

Dark Plum and Marrow Chutney

Preserves require forward planning, slow cooking and attention to the seasons. This makes the making of chutney, jams and jellies a weekend pastime for most back-late-from-work cooks. There is no better way of preserving the summer than getting involved with a box of jars and a mountain of late autumn harvest produce. Best of all is finding a bargain glut of some apples or some such on the market to make a batch of chutney to serve with cold meats and cheeses. The ideal is to make enough in the autumn to last you through to the following year. I've used fresh ginger here so that this chutney really sings, and muscovado sugar to give a real deep caramel taste.

Makes 6 x 500ml jars

900g onions
175g fresh root ginger
3 small dried chillies
2 teaspoons ground cinnamon
1 teaspoon ground cloves
800ml malt vinegar
900g golden plums
900g marrow
3 small eating apples
1 teaspoon salt
700g dark muscovado sugar

 You can substitute the marrow with extra plums if you wish, but the chutney will need longer to cook as there will be more moisture to evaporate..

Roughly chop the onions, and then place them in a food-processor and shred finely. Turn out into a really large saucepan. Peel and roughly chop the ginger and blitz in the food-processor in the same way. Add to the pan. Finely chop the dried chillies and add to the pan with the cinnamon and cloves. Splash in 200ml of the malt vinegar. Set the pan over a moderate heat and sweat the vegetables for 10 minutes, stirring occasionally until the mixture resembles a soft mush.

Meanwhile, stone the plums and roughly chop each one into about 8 pieces. Roughly peel the marrow, remove the seeds and cut into 2cm chunks. Peel and core the apples and then finely slice them. Add the plums, marrow, apples and salt to the pan and cook until soft – about 20 minutes. Add the remaining vinegar and turn the heat up high. Bring to a rumbling boil, and then turn down the heat slightly and boil for 35 minutes, stirring frequently. Remove from the heat.

Measure out the muscovado sugar and crumble it into the pan to break up the lumps. Bring the chutney back up to the boil, stirring all the time to stop it from sticking to the bottom of the pan, and then turn off the heat.

Sterilise your jars by filling them to the brim with boiling water. Drain. Carefully pour the hot chutney into the jars and seal immediately. Be careful – I once burnt my cleavage making chutney and it felt like piping hot lava.

Apple Russet Jelly

Making jelly is a bit like making jam, only it's lazier because you don't need to bother with all the preparation like pitting, stoning or peeling. You simply roughly chop your ingredients, sling them in a pot to cook, strain them overnight and then boil them up the next day to make the jelly. Russets are very old-fashioned apples with misty irregular peel and a wonderfully delicate flavour. I find they make for a lovely scented jelly, especially with the tint from the rose hips.

Makes 6 x 500ml jars

1.4kg russet apples, quartered
3 lemons, quartered
5cm piece of fresh root ginger, peeled and
   chopped
3 bay leaves
a handful of rose hips
a handful of fresh sage
granulated sugar

This jelly is perfect with cheese, just like membrillo (quince paste). I like it best with Monte Enebro. If you want to introduce a little kick, add some finely chopped chillies at the end.

Place the apples, lemons, ginger, bay leaves, rose hips, sage and 2.5 litres water in a large saucepan. Bring to the boil on a high heat, and then simmer for at least an hour until most of the apples have started to disintegrate.

Drape a 1m piece of untreated muslin over a large bowl. Pour the appley pulp into the muslin, and then tie up the corners to make a little bag. Suspend the bag over the bowl to catch the pectin-laden juices. If possible, leave to drip overnight.

The following morning, measure the drained liquid back into your saucepan. For every 600ml liquid you need to add 450g sugar. Place the pan back on the heat and bring the jelly back to the boil, stirring all the time until the sugar has dissolved. Once the sugar has dissolved, turn up the heat and boil rapidly until you reach setting point. To test the setting point, place a couple of saucers in the fridge to chill. Pour a spoonful of the liquid onto one of the cold saucers. Place this in the fridge for a few minutes. If it is at setting point, when you drag your finger over the surface of the syrup it will form a wrinkled film. Continue to test in quick succession so that you catch the right point. Skim off any scum with a spoon as it forms.

Meanwhile, sterilise your jars. Place a metal spoon inside each one and fill to the brim with boiling water. Place the lids in a bowl and pour over some boiling water to sterilise them too. Drain well.

Carefully pour the hot jelly into the sterilised jars and put on the lids straight away to make a natural seal. Store the jelly out of direct sunlight and keep in the fridge once opened.

Dark Marmalade

For as long as I can remember my mother has eaten the same breakfast daily: two small pieces of homemade bread, toasted, cooled, buttered and layered with her own marmalade, washed down with strong coffee. This is my breakfast of choice too when I have time. Tasting this makes me feel like I'm at home again. Recently, I've started to add star anise and fennel seeds to the mix to give the marmalade my own twist.

Makes 6 x 500ml jars

1.3kg Seville oranges
1 lemon
1 lime
2 teaspoons fennel seeds
8 whole star anise
7cm piece of fresh root ginger, peeled and
    cut into little matchsticks
2.7kg dark muscovado sugar

To sterilise the jars, pop a metal spoon inside the jar and then fill it to the brim with boiling water. To sterilise the lids, simply pour boiling water over those as well.

Scrub the Seville oranges if they are mucky and rinse well. Place in a really big saucepan with the lemon and lime and cover almost entirely with water. Place a lid on the pan and bring to the boil on a high heat. Simmer for about 15 minutes or until the fruit is soft. Leave until cool enough to handle, keeping the liquid. (If you wish, you can leave the fruit to cool overnight.)

Drape 1m untreated muslin over a large bowl ready for the fruit pulp. Remove the fruit from the pan using a slotted spoon. Don't throw away the cooking liquor. Slice the fruit in half, scoop out all of the flesh with a spoon and place in the muslin. Keep the skins to one side ready for slicing later. Put the fennel seeds in the muslin as well, and then tie up the corners to make a little bag. Place the muslin bag in a bowl to catch the juice.

Measure out 3.4 litres of the reserved cooking liquor into your largest saucepan. Add the muslin bag to the pan, along with any of the juice that has drained into the bowl. Drop the star anise into the pan and bring to the boil on a high heat. Boil rapidly for about an hour, or until the marmalade has reduced by half/two-thirds. Remove from the heat.

Meanwhile, cut up the peel quite finely so it is about 3mm thick. Once you have removed the pan from the heat, stir in the citrus peel and ginger. Suspend the muslin bag over the pan and leave to drain overnight. The following morning, add the sugar to the pan. Place the pan back on the heat and bring the marmalade slowly back to the boil, stirring all the time until the sugar has dissolved.

Once the sugar has dissolved, turn up the heat and boil rapidly until you reach setting point. To test that the marmalade is at setting point, place a couple of saucers in the fridge to chill. Scoop out a spoon of the marmalade liquid and pour onto one of the cold saucers. Place this in the fridge for a few minutes. If it is at setting point, when you drag your finger over the surface of the marmalade syrup it will form a wrinkled film. Continue to test in quick succession so that you catch the right point.

Once the marmalade has reached setting point, turn off the heat and leave it to stand for 10 minutes before jarring - this should prevent the peel from floating to the top of the jar. Fill the jars whilst the marmalade is still warm and put on the lids immediately to create a natural seal. I invested in a lovely metal funnel recently, specifically for making preserves, and it stops them spilling everywhere on the way into the jar.

Two Small Spelt Loaves

This recipe is perfect for a mildly productive afternoon. You can make the bread over the course of the day, stopping as you leave it to rise, so you can carry on with what you are doing. It leavens twice, once for an hour and again for a further half, so it's a lovely way of punctuating your day. The crescendo will be when you pull your loaves steaming out of the oven, hollow sounding and full of breakfast promise. Eat one during the week and pop the other in the freezer.

Makes 2 small loaves

500ml lukewarm water

1 tablespoon runny honey

14g dried active yeast

400g wholegrain spelt flour

250g strong white bread flour, plus extra for dusting

50g pumpkin seeds

1 teaspoon sea salt

 For variation you can swap the pumpkin seeds for sunflower seeds, linseeds, poppy seeds or even quinoa.

Mix together the water, honey and yeast in a measuring jug. Let this sit for 5 minutes until it develops a frothy surface. Measure out the flours, seeds and salt into a large wide bowl and pour in the yeast mixture. Gradually draw the flour into the liquid and mix to a pliable dough. Turn out onto a floured surface and knead for 10 minutes, pushing the dough in all directions until it becomes smooth and elastic and gives off a wheaty scent. Dust your original bowl with flour, pop the dough back inside and seal with an old plastic bag tied in a knot. Place the bowl somewhere warm like an airing cupboard and leave to rest for 1 hour until doubled in size. Meanwhile, grease and flour a large baking tray.

Dust your worksurface with flour, turn out the dough and knead again for 5 minutes to knock out all the air bubbles. Cut the dough in half and shape each piece into a small oval. Place on your prepared baking tray. Cover with a clean tea-towel and leave to prove in a warm place for 30 minutes. Preheat the oven to 220°C/gas mark 7.

Bake the loaves in the hot oven for an initial 15 minutes, and then turn down the heat to 190°C/gas mark 5 and cook for a further 35 minutes. Turn out onto a wire rack to cool completely. Store overnight in a plastic bag. Come morning, they will be perfect.

Saffron Scones

Scones are a staple British teatime treat, which apparently hail from Scotland. Traditionally they are served like a sandwich with clotted cream and jam, making for a really posh cream tea. The inclusion of saffron here, not only adds a beautiful golden tint to the scones but gives out a delicate scent, sweet like honey. Serve these with clotted cream and runny honey.

Makes 24

oil, for greasing
300ml whole milk
a pinch of saffron stems
120g butter
600g plain flour, plus extra for dusting
2 heaped teaspoons baking powder
1 teaspoon salt
½ teaspoon cinnamon
50g golden caster sugar
1 beaten egg (for the eggwash)
clotted cream and runny honey, to serve

Preheat the oven to 220°C/gas mark 7 and grease 2 baking sheets with oil. Measure the milk into a small pan. Add the saffron and set over a low heat to warm for 10 minutes. Set aside to infuse for 2 hours.

You can either use a food-processor to make the scones or do them by hand. Rub the butter into the flour until the mixture resembles fine breadcrumbs. Stir in the baking powder, salt, cinnamon and sugar. Using a knife, mix the infused milk into the dry ingredients, working quickly until it comes together in a slightly flaky ball. Don't overwork the dough. Tip out onto a floured worksurface and roll with a rolling pin until the dough is just shy of 2.5cm thick. Cut out 24 scones with a 6cm scone cutter and place on the greased baking trays. Brush each scone with the eggwash. Bake the scones, one tray at a time, in the hot oven for 15–20 minutes until golden and delicious.

Remove the first tray from the oven before you put in the second round of scones. Serve with clotted cream and a little drizzle of honey if you wish.

Scones are really versatile. Mum used to make them plain or with currants. I have made them with prunes and figs, variations worth giving a try.

A Big Caraway and Fennel Loaf

I owe my love of breadmaking to my mum, who still bakes two loaves a week. You can vary your loaves by adding a variety of ingredients: sunflower seeds, pumpkin seeds, linseeds and smaller spice seeds like caraway and fennel all work well. I particularly love caraway and fennel and have made a recipe here where their flavours can really, really sing.

Makes 1 big loaf

500ml lukewarm water
14g dried active yeast
2 teaspoons runny honey
600g strong white bread flour
100g wholemeal bread flour, plus extra
  for dusting
5g fennel seeds
5g caraway seeds
50g brown linseeds
1 teaspoon sea salt

This loaf is fantastically large and will keep you going for a few days so long as it is well wrapped in a paper bag.

Measure out the water into a jug and stir in the yeast and honey. Mix thoroughly and then place somewhere warm for about 10 minutes until bubbles start to appear on the surface. A radiator or airing cupboard is good in the winter, but come spring you can leave it in the garden in dappled sunlight.

Measure out the flours, seeds and salt into a wide, very large bowl. I use a Moroccan salad bowl. Pour the yeast mixture into the dry ingredients and begin to combine everything with your hands. It will be sloppy and stick to the bowl initially, but gradually it will form a dough ball. Turn out the dough onto a floured worksurface and knead for about 10 minutes. Dust your mixing bowl with a little flour and pop the dough back inside. Cover with a plastic bag and leave to rise somewhere warm for 30 minutes until doubled in size. Preheat the oven to 190°C/gas mark 5 and lightly dust a baking sheet with flour.

Turn out your dough onto a floured worksurface and knead for 5 minutes until soft and elastic. Shape into an oval and gently place on your baking sheet. Cover the loaf with a plastic bag and place somewhere warm to prove for about 40 minutes, or until doubled in size. When it has proved, slash into the surface. My mum does this by drawing a wheatear pattern into the tops of her loaves and they always look beautiful.

Carefully slide the baking tray into the oven, taking care not to knock out the air, and bake for 40–45 minutes. Remove to a wire rack to cool completely.

A Glazed Sunflower Tin

The first thing I did when we moved into our new flat was bake this loaf, a recipe I had been tweaking and evolving. Use a loaf tin to make a rectangular loaf or a large baking tray if you prefer an oval shape. The glaze creates a kitsch and satisfying look.

Makes 1 big loaf

a little butter, for greasing
500ml warm water
14g dried active yeast
2 teaspoons runny honey
300g strong white bread flour, plus extra
   for dusting
300g wholemeal flour
90g sunflower seeds
50g brown linseeds
1 heaped teaspoon sea salt
10g cornflour, for the glaze

 This bread is super-easy and you can do other stuff around the process, so it's perfect for a pottering day: do the first knead, do some weeding whilst the dough rises; do the next knead, ring around some friends for a Sunday catch-up; pop it in the oven, put your feet up!

Grease and lightly flour a 23cm loaf tin (or a large baking tray) and set aside. Mix together the warm water, yeast and honey in a jug and set aside for 5 minutes or so until the mixture begins to froth. Meanwhile, combine the flours, seeds and salt in a large, wide mixing bowl. Pour the yeasty mixture into the dry ingredients and gradually draw the flour into the liquid with your hands. Mix to a soft, pliable dough and then turn out onto a floured worksurface. Knead for at least 5 minutes – longer if possible. Dust your original mixing bowl with flour and pop the kneaded dough back inside. Cover with a cloth or an old shopping bag tied in a loose knot. Put the bowl in a warm place, such as an airing cupboard, and leave to rest for 45 minutes until doubled in size.

Tip your dough out onto a floured worksurface and knead again for 2–3 minutes to knock out the air bubbles. Shape the dough into an oblong and drop it into the prepared tin. Cover lightly with a cloth or bag and place the tin back in your warm place to prove for 30 minutes, or until doubled in size. Preheat the oven to 220°C/gas mark 7.

Once the loaf has risen, slash the top with a sharp knife, taking care not to knock out the air. Bake the loaf in the oven for an initial 10 minutes, and then turn down the heat to 190°C/gas mark 5 and bake for a further 40 minutes. To check the bread is cooked, turn it out of the tin immediately and tap the bottom – it should sound hollow. Place on a wire rack to cool.

Mix together the cornflour with 100ml water in a small pan. Heat very gently, whisking frequently, until the cornflour dissolves. Once it starts to bubble and become translucent, take the pan off the heat and brush the glaze all over the bread. Leave to dry. Eat for breakfast with some butter and homemade marmalade – and feel very smug!

Walnut Stuffed Tray-bake Bread

This bread provides a great and tasty bit of padding to a meal, particularly when you have extra mouths to feed. It makes a delicious meal for friends alongside some barbecued sausages and a dandelion salad (see page 39) or as part of a larger spread.

Serves 6

For the dough

300ml warm water

10g dried active yeast

1 teaspoon runny honey

530g strong white bread flour, plus extra for dusting

2 tablespoons olive oil, plus extra for greasing

1 teaspoon sea salt

For the topping

1 tablespoon cumin seeds

2 teaspoons rock salt, plus extra for the top

12 small sprigs fresh rosemary

40g walnuts

2 tablespoons olive oil

Measure out the warm water in a jug, add the yeast and honey and beat together thoroughly with a fork. Set aside somewhere warm for 10 minutes. Measure out the flour and place in a large mixing bowl. Pour in the yeast mixture, add the olive oil and salt and mix together with your hands to form a dough. Tip onto a floured worksurface and give the dough a good knead for 5–10 minutes (or use your mixer with the dough hook attached). Dust the bowl with a little flour and settle the dough back inside. Cover the bowl with a clean tea-towel, place near a radiator or in a warm room and leave to rest for 1 hour until doubled in size. This is your bread base.

To make the walnut topping, measure out the cumin seeds and rock salt into a pestle and mortar and pound and grind energetically to give a coarse powder. Add the rosemary and walnuts and grind again. Pour in the olive oil and mix to a paste. Set aside.

Preheat the oven to 180°C/gas mark 4. Grease a baking sheet with a little olive oil. Remove the dough from the bowl and knead for 3 minutes to knock out the air. Using a rolling pin, roll out the dough to form an oval sheet, 5mm thick. Rub the walnut paste over the middle of the dough, leaving a generous border clear around the edges. Using your hands, bring each of the 2 opposite sides into the centre, overlapping them slightly, so that you end up with a rectangle roughly 25 x 30cm. Give the filled dough another quick roll with your rolling pin to sandwich the layers together, and then transfer it to your oiled baking sheet. Cover with a tea-towel and set aside to prove for 20 minutes. Bake the bread in the oven for 30 minutes until light golden brown. Transfer to a wire rack to cool.

Tomato Tray-bake Bread

This is much like the Walnut Stuffed Tray-bake Bread on page 169. Having mastered the walnut version I wanted to play around with alternatives. I find myself frequently doing this. Run out of nuts? Plenty of tomatoes? Off you go. This is how my mother taught me to cook: learn a recipe, get it perfect, and then adapt it according to what you have to hand.

Serves 6

For the dough

300ml warm water

10g dried active yeast

1 teaspoon runny honey

530g strong white bread flour, plus extra
  for dusting

2 tablespoons olive oil, plus extra for
  greasing

a pinch of sea salt

For the topping

120g cherry tomatoes

5 garlic cloves, peeled and halved

6 sprigs of fresh rosemary

1 dried chilli, finely chopped (or
  ½ teaspoon chilli flakes)

2 tablespoons olive oil

2 teaspoons rock salt

Measure out the warm water in a jug, add the yeast and honey and beat together thoroughly with a fork. Set aside somewhere warm for 10 minutes. Measure out the flour and place in a large mixing bowl. Pour in the yeast mixture, add the olive oil and salt and mix together with your hands to form a dough. Tip onto a floured worksurface and give the dough a good knead for 5–10 minutes (or use your mixer with the dough hook attached). Dust the bowl with a little flour and settle the dough back inside. Cover the bowl with a clean tea-towel, place near a radiator or in a warm room and leave to rest for 1 hour until doubled in size. This is your bread base. Preheat the oven to 180°C/gas mark 4 and grease a 25 x 30cm baking sheet.

Flour your worksurface, tip out the dough and knead for 2–3 minutes to knock out the air. Roll out the dough using a rolling pin to fit your baking sheet and transfer to the baking sheet. Press the whole tomatoes and garlic all over the surface of the bread and then scatter with the rosemary and chilli. Drizzle with the olive oil and sprinkle with rock salt. Cover with a clean tea-towel and set aside to prove for 30 minutes. Bake in the oven for 30 minutes until the tomatoes are blistered and split and the bread is light golden brown. Remove to a wire rack to cool.

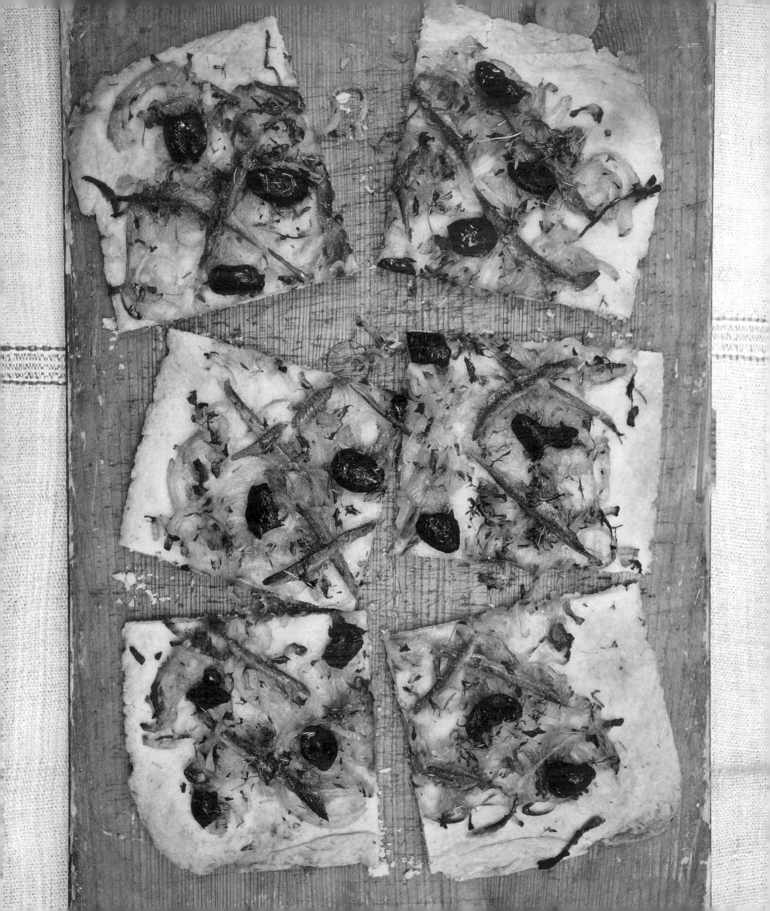

Pissaladière Two Ways

Pissaladière is the French take on pizza and you can buy it by the slice in bakeries all over France. The classic version consists of a dense layer of stringy sweet onions on a bread base, cross-hatched with salty anchovy fillets and punctuated with black olives. Being pretty much just onions, it is a bargain crowd-pleaser. I started making it a few years ago, and with nothing but leeks to hand ended up using this alternative allium family vegetable instead. Now I alternate between leeks and onions, depending on my mood. Take your pick.

Makes 6 big slices

120ml lukewarm water

15g dried active yeast

1 teaspoon caster sugar

250g plain flour, plus extra for dusting

90ml olive oil, plus 3 tablespoons

a pinch of sea salt

50g unsalted butter

1kg leeks (or 1kg onions)

a bunch of fresh thyme

6 anchovy fillets preserved in oil, sliced in
   half lengthways

12 pitted salty Provençal olives

Best eaten with hands (preferably at dusk whilst sitting on a doorstep!), it works really well served with a selection of salads – some dressed dandelion leaves, for example. If you want to keep to the French theme, serve it up with some cold meats and cheeses from the deli counter.

Measure out the water in a jug, stir in the yeast and sugar and leave to stand for 5 minutes or so. Meanwhile, measure out the flour into a large wide mixing bowl. Pour in the yeast mixture, add 90ml olive oil and season with a pinch of salt. Gradually draw the dry ingredients into the wet ingredients and mix to a pliable dough. Turn out onto a floured worksurface and knead for about 10 minutes, or until the dough is elastic and really pliable. When it is ready, flour the bowl, put the dough back inside, cover with clingfilm and leave to rise somewhere warm for about an hour, or until doubled in size.

Whilst your dough is rising, heat 3 tablespoons olive oil and the butter in a large saucepan over a moderate heat. Using a mandolin or food-processor, finely slice the leeks or onions – the finer the better. Add to the pan and turn down the heat to low. Sweat the onions/leeks for 20–30 minutes, stirring frequently, until they are really soft, stringy and transparent. Strip the leaves off the thyme and add half of them to the pan. Set aside whilst you finish off the base.

Preheat the oven to 220°C/gas mark 7. Oil a 25 x 30cm baking sheet with some olive oil. When your dough has doubled in size, tip it out onto a floured worktop and knead it for a few minutes to knock out the air. Roll out to fit your baking sheet and transfer to the baking sheet. Pile the leeks/onions onto the dough and spread them out so they are evenly distributed. Leave a crust around the edges. Slice the anchovies into wisps, arrange in a lattice pattern on top and press an olive into each diamond. Scatter over the rest of the thyme leaves and bake in the oven for 15–20 minutes. The onions should have developed a deep gold and the bread edges should be a sunny yellow.

Christmas Apple Tart

Serves 6–8

For the mincemeat (makes about 4 x 400g jars)

330g eating apples, peeled and grated
225g raisins
225g golden currants
225g Turkish sultanas
120g flaked almonds
2 teaspoons ground cinnamon
¼ whole nutmeg, grated
½ teaspoon ground mixed spice
zest and juice of 1 orange
juice of 1 lemon
100ml Sailor Jerry rum
200g runny honey, melted
225g butter, melted

For the pastry

350g plain flour, plus extra for rolling
175g unsalted butter
½ teaspoon sea salt
60ml cold water

For the tart

3 large eating apples (about 200g each),
   cored, peeled and diced
juice of half an orange
3 medium free-range eggs
284ml double cream
60ml whole milk
3 tablespoons caster sugar
4 tablespoons mincemeat
1 medium free-range egg, beaten

Contrary to the name, mincemeat is actually dried fruits and nuts, which have been jarred with spices and suet and preserved through the autumn to then stuff into pastry for Christmas day – sort of sweet mini-quiches. In an attempt to reinvent the minced pie, I came up with this alternative to bring a lighter twist to the classic. By using the mincemeat as a flavouring rather than the whole component, you get all the scents of Christmas but in a fresh apple pie. I have used my mum's vegetarian mincemeat, which although unorthodox, is delicious and light and nothing like the hefty shop-bought version.

To make the mincemeat, combine the grated apple, raisins, currants, sultanas, almonds, cinnamon, nutmeg, mixed spice and orange zest in a large mixing bowl. Then add lemon and orange juice and the rum. Thoroughly mix and set aside.

In a small pan on a low heat, melt together the honey and butter. When it is liquid, pour this over the mincemeat mix. Pot in sterilised jars, packing it tightly down before sealing. Set aside to steep somewhere dark and cool for a few weeks.

You will need a 23cm tart tin with a loose bottom. Preheat the oven to 220°C/gas mark 7. To make the pastry, measure out the flour, butter and salt into a large mixing bowl. Using a knife, continually cut the butter until you have something that resembles breadcrumbs and is light. Pour in the cold water and continue to work with a knife for just long enough for the pastry to draw together. When it is a big ball, turn it out onto a floured worktop. Using a floured rolling pin work the pastry into a large circle, bigger than your tart tin. Roll the pastry onto your rolling pin and then reverse the roll out over your tin. Press the pastry into the edges of the tin and then roll your pin over the sides to perfectly slice the excess pastry off. Keep this excess for the later lattice. Line the pastry tin with greaseproof paper and pour in some baking beans. Place in the preheated oven for 5 minutes. Remove the baking beans and paper and return to the oven for just long enough for the base

to dry out (usually about 2 minutes). Remove the tart from the oven to cool and reduce the temperature to 160°C/gas mark 3.

For the apple tart, place apples in a medium pan with the orange juice. Heat with the lid on over a low heat for a few minutes to soften the fruit. Remove from the heat and set aside. Beat together the eggs, double cream, milk and caster sugar. Return to your pastry case. Scatter over the par-cooked apples and then add the mincemeat. Pour most of the beaten custard over this, keeping a third aside. Place the tart in the oven, and pull out the shelf. Pour the rest of the custard in and gently push the shelf back in. This dramatically reduces the chance of the custard leaking over the edge of the tin. Bake in the oven for 25 minutes.

Roll the remaining pastry into a long wide strip and then cut into thumb-width ribbons. Remove the tart from the oven and lattice the pastry over the half-cooked tart and brush with some beaten egg. Return the tart to the oven for a further 20 minutes. If when the tart is cooked (doesn't wobble any more) the lattice is not quite golden you can place it under a medium grill for a few minutes to get the ultimate effect.

Banana Caramel Tart

This tart comes all the way from my primary school, where it was a weekly delight on the menu in the guise of the 'gypsy tart'. Indeed it is known as a school dinners dish and was really popular in the 1970s and 1980s. Cut the saccharine taste with some crème fraîche or natural yogurt for light relief. I have added an uncharacteristic shot of coffee which serves to deepen the caramel flavours.

Serves 6–8

For the tart
300g plain flour, plus extra for dusting
150g butter
2 tablespoons cold water
410g can evaporated milk
350g dark muscovado sugar
20ml (1 shot) of strong espresso coffee
1 large egg
a pinch of sea salt

For the caramelised bananas
150g golden caster sugar
40g butter, diced
5 firm bananas, cut into thumb-width
   discs

crème fraîche, to serve

Preheat the oven to 220°C/gas mark 7. Place the flour and butter in a mixing bowl and, using 2 knives, mix until it resembles fine breadcrumbs. Alternatively, use a food-processor or your own hands. Add the cold water a little at a time to draw the pastry together. Shape into a ball, but do not overwork it, and turn out onto a floured worktop. Dust the pastry with flour and roll out until it is slightly larger than your tart tin. Lift the pastry up, supporting it over your rolling pin, and flip it into the tin. Gently press into the corners with your fingertips and then roll the pin over the top to slice away any excess pastry. Line the pastry case with baking parchment and fill with baking beans. Bake in the oven for 10 minutes and then remove the baking beans and parchment. Return to the oven for a further 3–5 minutes – just long enough to dry out the base. Remove, set aside and turn the heat down to 190°C/gas mark 5.

Combine the evaporated milk, sugar, coffee, egg and salt in a bowl. Using a hand mixer, work the mixture for 15 minutes until it forms a thick foam – it takes this long to get the texture perfect. Place the pastry case back in the oven, pull out the shelf and carefully pour the caramel into the tin. Ease the shelf back into the oven and leave to bake for 15 minutes. The surface should be slightly tacky when you remove it and there should still be a bit of a wobble in the middle that will set as it cools. If necessary, you can leave it in the oven for a further 5 minutes.

To make the caramelised banana topping, heat the caster sugar in a non stick frying pan on a low heat. Do not stir. When it is molten and liquid, remove from the heat and drop in the butter. Swirl the pan as you would with a tarte tatin until the caramel is homogenous, and then add the bananas. Return the pan to a low heat and toss the bananas gently for a few minutes until they are coated and delicious. To serve, cut the tart into wedges, spoon over the caramelised bananas and accompany with a dollop of crème fraîche.

Pastel de Chocolate Oaxaqueno

The framework for this recipe comes from Elizabeth David's classic dark chocolate cake. After a recent trip to Mexico I started to think about how I could adapt her recipe to make it deeper and more Latin. In the Day of the Dead market in Oaxaca, I drank a delicious and really cinnamony hot chocolate with 'churros' so for this recipe I've twisted and tweaked Elizabeth David's original version to include the heady, dark smells and volcanic mountains of mole that dominate this honestly joyous market.

Serves 6

150g unsalted butter, plus a little extra for greasing

200g dark chocolate (at least 70 per cent cocoa solids)

1 x 20ml shot of espresso

1 x 20ml shot of Marsala

150g dark muscovado sugar

2 teaspoons ground cinnamon, plus extra for dusting

1 teaspoon cayenne pepper, plus extra for dusting

20g desiccated coconut

90g ground almonds

5 large free-range eggs, separated

ricotta, to serve

Butter a 20cm round, loose-bottomed cake tin and preheat the oven to 180°C/gas mark 4. Measure out the chocolate, coffee, Marsala, sugar and butter into a mixing bowl. Place the bowl over a pan of gently simmering water and stir until everything is melted and homogenous. Take your time doing this. Beat in the cinnamon and cayenne pepper, and then taste the mixture to check you are happy with the spicing. Finally, stir in the desiccated coconut, ground almonds and egg yolks.

Place the whites in a separate, clean mixing bowl and whisk until stiff peaks form. Using a slotted spoon, gently fold a spoonful of the whites into the chocolate batter to loosen it. Now gently fold in the rest of the whites, being careful to maintain the lightness. Turn the mixture out into the buttered cake tin and bake in the oven for 55 minutes until it is raised and cracked on top like an arid landscape. Leave to cool and set in the tin for a few hours, and then turn out onto a wire rack. Dust with cinnamon and a little cayenne. In the absence of requesón (Mexican fresh strained cheese), serve with a spoonful of soft ricotta.

Real Raspberry Cupcakes

Cupcakes have become a really fashionable form of sugar. They are pretty as peaches when they are done well and the essence of these cakes are the mountainous waves of icing that crown every high-street bakery. Famously synthetic, gaudily decorated, the cupcake is a force to be reckoned with. I started making cupcakes after a sojourn around Australia. Their cupcakes differ from the British variety, beautifully executed and yet earthy and natural too. This is where I picked up this very icing and also another one with passion fruit seeds. This one is gaudy and pink and yet entirely natural and raspberry-ish.

Makes 12

For the cupcakes
115g unsalted butter
180g golden caster sugar
3 large free-range eggs
a few drops of vanilla extract
210g self-raising flour
a pinch of salt

For the icing
70g fresh raspberries
400g icing sugar, sieved
gold balls and frosted flowers, to decorate

Preheat the oven to 170°C/gas mark 3 ½. Line a 12-hole muffin tray with paper cases – I like the brown ones most. Partly melt the butter in a small pan, mixing with a whisk until it is a soft molten butter. Remove from the heat and spoon into a large mixing bowl. Add the sugar and beat with an electric hand mixer until super-smooth and creamy. Beat in the eggs one at a time. Wait for each of the eggs to be incorporated before adding the next and keep beating until smooth. Using a large, metal spoon, fold in the vanilla, flour and salt. Spoon the mixture into the paper cases so that they are three-quarters full. Bake in the oven for 15 minutes until they are firm, and then remove to a wire rack to cool.

To make the icing, weigh the raspberries into a bowl with tall sides (to stop you getting splattered). Using a hand mixer, beat well until the raspberries have broken down to a liquid. Gradually add the icing sugar and whisk until you have a thick paste. Decorate the cakes with the pink icing, using a small palette knife dipped in boiling water to spread the icing like butter, rather than piping it. Decorate immediately with cake decorations – if you leave it too long, the icing with develop a seal and nothing will stick. Now put the kettle on…

Sapota Upside-down Cake

This is an alternative to the old winter favourite, pineapple upside-down cake. Sapota is a grainy, sticky fruit that is native to Mexico and the Caribbean, and it is available tinned from West Indian shops. Of course, there are other wintery fruits you could use in its place. Cranberries are amazing too. In fact, last time I made a cranberry upside-down cake for Christmas it hardly touched the table before my friends finished it.

Serves 8

190g unsalted butter
500g canned sapota (available from West Indian stores)
190g golden caster sugar
1 tablespoon flower honey
3 large free-range eggs
150g self-raising flour
40g ground almonds
yogurt and runny honey, to serve

Preheat the oven to 180°C/gas mark 4 and line a 22cm round cake tin with greaseproof paper. Melt 50g of the butter in a small pan and pour over the base of the cake tin. Drain the fruit and arrange beautifully in the bottom of the tin. Sprinkle all over with 50g of the caster sugar and drizzle with honey.

To make the cake, cream the remaining 140g butter with the remaining 140g sugar. I like to use a hand mixer for this. Add the eggs, one at a time, beating well between each addition. Gradually fold in the flour and almonds (which add extra moisture to your fruit cake) and then spread the mixture evenly over your fruit – try not to mess up your design. Bake in the oven for an initial 30 minutes, and then turn down the oven to 150°C/gas mark 2 and bake for a further 30 minutes. Leave the cake to cool in the tin for 20 minutes before cutting into wedges. Serve with a dollop of yogurt and a drizzle of honey for extra exoticism.

My Lime and Cardamom Drizzle Cake

I make a version of this cake at least once a week. It's a recipe I know off by heart and one that I love dearly. Each time I make it I change it slightly according to my mood. I wrote the original recipe for my first book. Light, flourless and nutty this later incarnation is full of the Indian scents of verdant cardamom and sharp lime.

Serves 8

butter, for greasing
200g ground almonds
300g golden caster sugar
6 medium free-range eggs
3 limes
2 teaspoons ground cardamom

Grease a 25cm round, loose-bottomed cake tin and preheat the oven to 160°C/gas mark 3. In a mixing bowl, measure out the ground almonds, 200g of the caster sugar and 3 of the eggs. Using a wooden spoon beat well to form a thick paste. Separate the remaining 3 eggs. Add the yolks to the cake mixture and place the whites in a separate mixing bowl. Zest the limes and add to the cake mixture along with the cardamom. (Set aside the zested limes for later.) Using a clean whisk, beat the egg whites until stiff peaks form. Using a slotted spoon, carefully fold the whites into the cake mixture, taking care not to knock out any of the air. Using a spatula, scrape the cake mixture into your greased tin and bake in the oven for 1 hour.

To make the drizzle, squeeze the juice of all 3 limes into a small saucepan. Add the remaining 100g sugar and warm on a low heat to dissolve completely. Remove the cake from the oven and immediately pour over the lime drizzle. Set aside to cool in the tin and absorb the drizzle before transferring to a wire rack to cool completely. Dust with the ground cardamom.

The Best Lemon and Lime Drizzle Cake

My friend Sophie Moody makes the best lemon drizzle cake – so much so that everyone rejoices when she comes over because she is usually armed with one. It is such a cosy cake. Sophie's drizzle cake recipe originally came from *Cranks*, who made lots of cookbooks in the late 1970s and early 1980s. I think this recipe resonates hugely with me because my mum loves *Cranks* recipes too. Like me, Sophie changes this recipe from time to time and plays around with the ingredients. You don't need to add the poppy seeds, or you could use just lemons or just limes. In honour of this constant evolution, I have added an additional icing to her famous recipe to give extra sour clout.

Serves 8

125g butter, plus extra for greasing
2 lemons
1 lime
225g golden caster sugar, plus
    3 teaspoons
3 large free-range eggs
200g self-raising flour
4 teaspoons natural yogurt
1 tablespoon poppy seeds, plus a pinch
    for the top
190g icing sugar, sieved

Preheat the oven to 180°C/gas mark 4 and thoroughly grease a 30cm loaf tin. Beat the butter in a mixing bowl with a hand mixer until it is soft. Grate in the zest of one of the lemons and the lime. (Keep the fruit aside for later.) Beating continuously, gradually add 225g caster sugar. Beat in the eggs one at a time. Discard your mixer in favour of a spatula and carefully fold in the flour, making sure you reach right to the bottom to combine it fully. Finally, mix in the yogurt and poppy seeds. Turn the batter out into your greased loaf tin and bake in the oven for 45 minutes. When it is cooked through, a toothpick will come out of the cake clean.

To make the drizzle topping, squeeze the juice of the zested lemon and lime into a small saucepan and add the remaining 3 teaspoons caster sugar. Heat over a low heat until the sugar has dissolved, and then pour immediately over the cake. Sophie suggests making a few holes with a toothpick to further allow the syrup to sink into the cake. Set aside for 20 minutes to cool in the tin and absorb the syrup.

When your cake is cool, turn it out onto a wire rack to cool completely. To make the icing, zest the second lemon into a measuring jug and stir in the icing sugar and the remaining lemon juice. Beat well to remove any lumps and then pour half of the icing over the cake. Spread out to the edges with a palette knife before pouring over the remainder. Sprinkle with a few more poppy seeds and leave to set before serving.

Apricot and Ginger Upside-down Cake

Upside-down cake is a great way of using up surplus fruit and making something fresh tasting for tea. The best bit is where the cake batter meets the fruit, where it is all gooey and tinged with the colour of summer – wet and moreish. This uses fresh fruit, so it is a summer cake, but see page 182 for a version with tinned fruit for when there's little on the market stalls. I've used some brown flour in this recipe which balances the wet, tart, jammy fruit with a wholemeal element. As it is a shallow cake, deep with fruit like its close French cousin tarte tatin, it is best served warm with some double cream on the side. Serve it up for pudding after a summer lunch.

Serves 8

200g unsalted butter

60g granulated sugar

400g firm apricots, halved and stoned

150g golden caster sugar

zest of ½ lemon

a few drops of vanilla extract

5cm piece of fresh root ginger, peeled and grated

3 medium free-range eggs

80g wholemeal flour

70g self-raising flour

½ teaspoon baking powder

double cream, to serve

Grease the sides of a 25cm round cake tin, and line the base with greaseproof paper. Preheat the oven to 180°C/gas mark 4. Smudge 60g of the butter over the base of the tin and sprinkle with 30g granulated sugar. Arrange the apricots over the base of the tin in an even mosaic, using the butter as glue. Sprinkle over the rest of the granulated sugar and set the tin to one side.

To make the sponge, beat together the remaining 140g butter with the caster sugar. I use a hand mixer for this. When it is pale and light, add the lemon zest, vanilla extract and ginger and beat until smooth. Crack in all 3 eggs at the same time and beat well. Add the flours and baking powder and beat until smooth. Spread the cake mixture over the apricot base and bake in the oven for an initial 25 minutes. Turn the heat down to 150°C/gas mark 2 and bake for a further 30 minutes until pale golden brown. If you plunge a toothpick into the centre it should come out clean. Remove the cake from the oven and let it stand in its tin for 20 minutes before turning it out, upside down, onto a nice plate. Serve warm with some double cream on the side.

 What you choose to add to your upside-down cake is entirely up to you – and will probably depend on your mood and the season. Rhubarb and ginger is another lovely variation.

Walnut and Coffee Loaf Cake with Cracked Beans and Mascarpone Icing

One of my mum's fallback cakes was coffee and walnut. I vividly remember the bottle of 'Camp' coffee that stood inviting and proud in the larder, ready for weekend baking. My mum's version uses a time-honoured Victoria sponge recipe and then adds this chicory tincture. It has a flavour which is like coffee, but also has an identity all of its own. Failing to find 'Camp', I've used instant coffee here. I love the slightly synthetic coffee flavour, but have zooped it up by scattering real coffee beans over the cream cheese icing for the sake of modernity.

Serves 8

220g unsalted butter, plus extra for greasing
220g golden caster sugar
4 large free-range eggs
220g self-raising flour
a pinch of salt
1 heaped tablespoon instant coffee granules
1 tablespoon boiling water
75g walnuts, roughly chopped
100g mascarpone
400g icing sugar
1 tablespoon whole coffee beans

Preheat the oven to 180°C/gas mark 4 and grease a 30cm loaf tin. Bring the butter to room temperature, so that it is soft, and then measure it into a large mixing bowl. Add the sugar and beat together until creamy and pale. I like to do this with an electric hand mixer. Add the eggs, one at a time, and beat well to form a really smooth batter. Using a large metal spoon, carefully fold in the flour and salt. Mix the coffee granules with the boiling water to make a seriously strong little shot of coffee and fold into the cake mixture with the walnuts. Spoon the mixture into your loaf tin and bake in the oven for 45 minutes. To check that it is cooked through, insert a toothpick in the middle of the cake. Leave it for a moment and then withdraw it – it should come out clean of cake mix. Transfer the cake to a wire rack to cool for 3 hours.

To make the icing, beat together the mascarpone and icing sugar. Using a bendy knife or palette knife, spread the icing over the top of the cake. To make the coffee topping, crack the coffee beans in a pestle and mortar and scatter them over the iced cake.

Hot Ginger Cake

This is my mum's current favourite and it's a sure-fire winner. It has a wonderful fine, dense texture because the batter is hot before baking (a great trick). Mum does it with currants, but I prefer a topping of fresh or crystallised ginger. Take your pick.

Serves 10

225g butter, plus extra for greasing
225g treacle
225g muscovado sugar
225g self-raising flour
1 teaspoon baking powder
3 teaspoons good ground ginger
1 large free-range egg
50ml boiling water
7.5cm piece of fresh root ginger, peeled
  and sliced into matchsticks

Preheat the oven to 180°C/gas mark 4 and grease a 25cm round, loose-bottomed cake tin. Measure out the butter, treacle and muscovado into a large saucepan and place on a low heat. Using a wooden spoon, stir the mixture until the sugar has dissolved and you are left with a molten gooey mass. Remove from the heat and set aside to cool for 5–10 minutes.

Add the self-raising flour, baking powder and ground ginger to the pan and beat thoroughly to make sure there are no lumps. Beat in the egg and finally stir in the boiling water to loosen the mixture. Turn out into your prepared tin and scatter over the fresh ginger pieces. Bake in the oven for 1 hour. It should have a tacky surface and be a little sunken in the middle. Allow the cake to cool in the tin for 30 minutes before turning it out onto a wire rack to cool completely.

Index

Author Acknowledgements

The biggest thanks goes of course to my mum for teaching me how to cook.

But also to my whole family who constantly support me and do nothing but talk about food!

Thanks also to all the friends who have added recipes to my kitchen, and eaten at our table.

Thanks to my husband for putting up with my endless chatter and constant hunger.

And a massive thanks to Kyle Cathie for giving me the opportunity to write this book and Vicky Orchard for her patient editing.